From one of today's foremost thinkers on church movements, *What Actually Starts Movements* brings together compelling research, personal experiences, and farsighted vision to show how leaders can take their ministries to the next level. Emanuel Prinz goes beyond mere platitudes and digs deeply into years of data to find out how leaders can maximize the tools at their disposal to start and sustain major movements for God. Anyone wishing to develop into the type of leader that moves boldly and makes change should read this book.

DAVE FERGUSON, author, *Hero Maker* and *B.L.E.S.S.*; CEO, Exponential

Emanuel Prinz has done a great service to the body of Christ in researching the characteristics of church-planting movement catalysts. I'm grateful for his contribution to our understanding of the qualities that God cultivates in his servants that can contribute to movements that are reaching the world for Jesus Christ.

DR. DAVID GARRISON, author, *Church Planting Movements*

As a disciple-making movement practitioner and catalyst in many places, I have observed what Emanuel Prinz shares with us in his book. This book is a treasure for those who want to start, multiply, and sustain disciple-making movements in many places. I'm sure as you pursue God's purpose in making disciples, the lessons, ideas, and experiences shared in this book will change your approach to ministry and help you launch sustainable disciple-making movements.

May you be blessed as you learn and help others learn how to make and multiply disciples.

DR. AILA TASSE, founder, Lifeway Global; regional director, East/Southern Africa, New Generations

Emanuel Prinz is a frustrating writer! He leaves no stone unturned, is deeply thoughtful, and always attempts to stay close to the biblical text and the facts on the ground. He makes it hard to disagree with him, yet you might, as even I do at times. BUT you will not regret one minute of the time you invest in this book. Whether you buy its conclusions or disagree vehemently, you will be better for having submitted yourself to Prinz's careful analysis, unbounded mind, and soft heart. That trilogy makes him dangerous to your thinking.

ROY MORAN, chairman, board of directors, New Generations; author, *Spent Matches*

This book will help you know where to start. It is timely and beneficial in our work at Experience Life. We all would do well to pay attention.

CHRIS GALANOS, founding pastor, Experience Life Church, Lubbock, Texas; author, *From Megachurch to Multiplication*

Emanuel Prinz has so expertly mapped out the terrain of movements. This book is a treasure trove of insights and profoundly practical. I find it deeply resonant.

ALAN HIRSCH, award-winning author/coauthor of numerous books on missional spirituality, leadership, and organization; cofounder, Movement Leaders Collective, the Forge Missional Training Network, and 5Q Collective

Emanuel Prinz's *What Actually Starts Movements* is a groundbreaking work, providing clarity and rigor to the critical question of what fuels and sustains disciple-making movements. Backed by empirical research, Prinz identifies the essential traits and practices of effective catalytic leaders, emphasizing the importance of the right person over mere methodology. The insights offered in this book have the potential to reshape missiological strategies and empower leaders committed to the "healing of the nations" through Christ. This is an important resource for practitioners and scholars dedicated to seeing movements of disciples multiply worldwide.

DR. WES WATKINS, facilitator, Motus Dei Network; adjunct professor, Trinity Evangelical Divinity School

I first met Emanuel Prinz in the 1990s in Sudan when he was a young visionary. Little did we both know how God was going to use him in Sudan to see an unprecedented, mind-blowing number of Muslims come to Christ. I myself was once deeply impacted by a statement from Colton Weerasingha, an apostolic father figure from Sri Lanka, who declared, "God's method is a person. Are you that person?" I found myself sitting on the beach in Colombo, crying out to God, "Allow me to be that person!"

Now, Prinz is telling you the very same thing, bolstered by amazing research, facts, and figures—and a life to prove it. But look, once you are through with the book, find that beach and pray the same. Heaven is the limit to what will happen.

WOLFGANG SIMSON, author, *Houses that Change the World* and *The Constitution of the Kingdom*

In *What Actually Starts Movements*, Emanuel Prinz has identified a bundle of movement boosters and movement blockers worthy of consideration for anyone trying to launch a new disciple-making movement (DMM). I believe Prinz would be the first to say there are no hard and fast rules, but that's part of the magic of a comprehensive book like this one. It spawns discussion and makes all of us rethink our positions. You'll want to read this book—it will end up making all of us better.

DR. DOUG LUCAS, president, Team Expansion; author, *More Disciples*

I LOVE this book! It is a deep well of research-backed insight and an inspiring rallying cry for movemental Christianity and the catalytic leadership needed to spark movements. As a reader, you will be both informed and inspired. Prinz demystifies what it takes to become the kind of leader God uses to spark movements, offering a solid foundation and practical framework for growing into that role. He shares core movement boosters and blockers and the vital characteristics for us to learn from and to grow in. A masterclass—and a must-read for anyone passionate about the church in our current moment.

RICH ROBINSON, cofounder, Movement Leaders Collective and Creo; author, *All Change*

What could I possibly learn from another book—after reading a flood of movement books and spending decades as a hands-on practitioner, trainer, and coach of real leaders facilitating real movements? A lot! Prinz isn't just writing from theory—he's an actual practitioner. And yes, he brings a bit of that academic Teutonic edge. His research backs up, with scholarly rigor, what the Spirit has been whispering to us for years: God uses people—especially a certain kind of person. As a wise saint once said, "Men search for methods; God searches for a man (or person)."

Prinz documents the kind of person the Lord tends to smile on. But this is not one of those books that suggests, "Just be like this and fruit is automatic." That would be as shallow as others that imply, "Use this strategy with these tools and success is guaranteed." Movements don't work like that—and God doesn't work like that.

What makes this book so valuable is that Prinz sets a mark—he describes the kind of person God consistently chooses to use, and ministry approaches that are empirically present in actual movements. He isn't offering a formula— he's showing us the real-life traits and practices that align with how God tends to work when movements happen. He gives us insight into who we need to become and what we need to be doing if we long to see the gospel sweep through a people with Book-of-Acts impact. If God has stirred your heart to be a disciple-maker, start here. If he's called you to reach a people group, start here.

BILL SMITH, "The Father of Movements"

Emanuel Prinz has gifted us with a significant contribution to the study of movements. *What Actually Starts Movements* is a thoroughly researched and data-driven exploration that reveals not only how movements begin but also what sustains them. Drawing on extensive global fieldwork and analysis, Prinz demonstrates with clarity the vital role of catalytic leadership and the spiritual posture necessary for multiplication. More than a technical manual, this book draws readers into the Father's heart, reminding us that movements are not merely strategic but deeply relational. The questions at the end of each chapter serve as thoughtful guides for reflection and practical application, making this an invaluable resource for both practitioners and scholars.

DR. MICHAEL T. COOPER, author, *Ephesiology*

Since the birth of the church, God has given to the body of believers, the person and power of the Holy Spirit for his work on this earth. Those of us who profess to be Christ-followers of the living generations need to be both pure of heart and savvy, even shrewd, in optimizing all the resources that we have. This book, through careful research, identifies those catalytic patterns, traits, and strategies and reminds us that our God is the living God, catalytic, always moving, calling the lost unto himself. It also calls us into alignment with the heart, movement, and plan of God so that what we do with the days he has given us truly lasts for eternity.

REV. DR. LISA PAK, Finishing the Task Partners and Networks

Emanuel Prinz's inspiring book hearkens us back to the early church, ignited and led by intrepid men and women who embodied deep prayer, assertive love, and expectant faith. They dared to defy convention to follow the Holy Spirit's own transformational disciple-making. Based on meticulous research of 147 movements worldwide, Prinz captures the essential qualities of the "who," instead of the methodologies of the "what." This broadest-ever movement book also serves as a practical spiritual formation on cultivating these catalytic characteristics. And while growing in these twenty-one catalytic traits, we find that in the process we become more and more like the Jesus we love, follow, and serve.

DR. MARY HO, international executive leader, All Nations

From the inception of Christianity, the Great Commission and the message of the gospel have been intrinsically linked to the concept of Jesus' incarnation within the community. God's movement is much like the sun's gradual ascent to its zenith, dispelling the darkness of all kinds. *What Actually Starts Movements* is an excellent research work by Emanuel Prinz. I highly recommend this book to anyone interested in studying and understanding movements.

VICTOR JOHN, movement catalyst; author,
Bhojpuri Breakthrough and *Breakthrough Leadership*

When I received a copy of Emanuel Prinz's new book, I couldn't wait to dive in. I was so captivated that I finished it the same day, unable to put it down. In this invaluable resource, he blends rigorous global research with deeply practical insights. His analysis of 147 movements across diverse cultural contexts provides actionable strategies grounded in real-world experiences that partner with God. What sets this book apart is its dual emphasis on the spiritual qualities of a catalytic leader and the practical methods that nourish movements. Each chapter provides clear steps, reflective exercises, and growth pathways, making it both inspiring and highly applicable. Whether you are a pioneer church planter, a ministry leader, or a trainer, this book equips you to evaluate your own leadership, refine your methodological strategies, and grow into the kind of servant that God can use to catalyze transformative, multiplicative movements.

DR. MATT FRETWELL, Lausanne Church Planting Catalyst; professor, Regent University; author, *Church Planting*

WHAT ACTUALLY STARTS MOVEMENTS

EMANUEL PRINZ

WHAT ACTUALLY STARTS MOVEMENTS

Partnering with God for Kingdom Multiplication

100 MOVEMENTS PUBLISHING

First published in 2025 by 100 Movements Publishing
www.100Mpublishing.com

Library of Congress Control Number: 2025908310

ISBN (print): 978-1-955142-66-3
ISBN (ebook): 978-1-955142-67-0

Cover Design by Jude May
Cover image © JamesBrey | iStock

100 Movements Publishing
An imprint of Movement Leaders Collective
Cody, Wyoming
www.movementleaderscollective.com

TO MY ABBA FATHER
Without your boundless compassion,
I would not be in ministry today,
nor would this book have been written.

TO ANNA
You are a daily reflection of the Father's
tender affection and love.

CONTENTS

FOREWORD

Alan Hirsch

Movements. The very word evokes a sense of dynamic energy, a surge of life, and the prospect of transformative change. Yet, as those of us who have labored in the field of missional leadership and apostolic engagement know, movements do not just happen. They are not the product of happenstance or sheer enthusiasm. They require a convergence of the right conditions, the right strategies, and—most crucially—the right people. This is the terrain that Dr. Emanuel Prinz has so expertly mapped out in *What Actually Starts Movements*.

Emanuel's book represents a highly significant contribution to the study and practice of movement dynamics. As someone who has spent decades exploring the DNA of movements—what I often refer to as "movemental thinking"—I find his work deeply resonant. He doesn't just theorize; he interrogates reality. Drawing from his empirical research into 147 movements across the globe, Emanuel brings both rigor and relevance to the conversation. This is no small feat. In an era awash with oversimplified how-to guides and reductive formulas, Emanuel offers us something far more substantial: a robust synthesis of data, story, and actionable insight.

At the heart of this book lies a crucial paradigm shift—one that movement thinkers have long intuited but which Emanuel substantiates with compelling clarity. It's not just about methods. Methods matter, yes, but only insofar as they are employed by the right kind of person. The catalytic leader, with their unique blend of traits and competencies, is the linchpin of any movement. Emanuel's research underscores this point with startling precision. He identifies twenty-one specific qualities that distinguish effective catalysts from those who fall short of sparking lasting change—traits such as deep prayer, expectant faith, and an assertiveness tempered by love.

What struck me most in reading this book is the way Emanuel frames these traits within the broader ecology of movemental dynamics. He doesn't present them as isolated virtues to be pursued for their own sake but as integral components of a holistic approach to leadership and discipleship. This resonates deeply with my own emphasis on APEST (apostles, prophets, evangelists, shepherds, and teachers, as outlined in Ephesians 4:1–16) as a framework for understanding the roles and functions necessary for the health and growth of the body of Christ. The catalytic leader, in Emanuel's account, embodies the apostolic impulse—a relentless drive to pioneer, innovate, and empower others for multiplication.

One of the standout sections of the book is Emanuel's discussion on prayer. He challenges the prevailing notion that sheer volume—"much prayer"—is the key to movemental breakthrough. Instead, he points us to what he calls "deep prayer"—a prayer life marked by intimacy with God, attentiveness to his voice, and a profound alignment with his purposes. This is the kind of prayer that fuels not just activity but also transformation, both in the leader and in the communities they serve. It's a timely reminder that movements are, at their core, a work of the Spirit. Our role, as Emanuel so aptly puts it, is to partner with God, not to manufacture results through human striving.

Another highlight is Emanuel's emphasis on the role of influencing others' beliefs. In a world increasingly resistant to change, the ability to inspire, persuade, and challenge deeply held assumptions is a critical competency for any movement leader. Emanuel illustrates this with powerful examples from his own experience, showing how catalytic leaders create environments where transformation becomes not just possible but almost inevitable.

This book is not just a treasure trove of insights; it is also profoundly practical. Most chapters conclude with actionable steps, reflective exercises, and guiding questions designed to help readers grow into the kind of leaders God can use to catalyze movements. Whether you are a seasoned practitioner or just beginning to explore the world of movements, you will find in these pages both a roadmap and a source of inspiration.

As I read, I found myself thinking of the early church—the quintessential movement that turned the world upside down. What made it so potent, so resilient, so generative? It wasn't just their methods—though those were remarkable. It was their deep dependence on God, their boldness in the face of opposition, and their relentless commitment to the mission of Jesus. These are the same qualities that Emanuel identifies in today's catalytic leaders. And they are the qualities he shows us how to cultivate in our own lives and ministries.

In *What Actually Starts Movements*, Emanuel Prinz has given us a gift. He has distilled years of research, reflection, and real-world experience into a book that is as inspiring as it is instructive. More than that, he has reminded us that the call to catalyze movements is not reserved for a select few. It is an invitation extended to all who dare to follow Jesus into the wild and unpredictable adventure of mission.

So, as you turn these pages, may you do so with an open heart and a willing spirit. May you hear the call to partner with God in his redemptive work. And may you find, as so many have, that the journey toward movemental impact begins not with a method but with a person—someone like you. Someone willing to say, "Here I am. Send me."

FOREWORD

Chris Galanos

I walked into the Embassy Suites hotel in Denton, TX, just after the ending of the Global Alliance for Church Multiplication (GACX) conference in 2023. I had come to meet several Thai pastors who were at the conference. Little did I know I'd get the opportunity to meet someone else whose work I had admired for quite some time.

Dr. Emanuel Prinz happened to be sitting in the lobby while I was meeting with the Thai pastors. I was excited to be able to shake his hand and thank him for his influence. I had read journal articles he had written, and I also subscribe to his blog. Since that first encounter, we have become friends.

I think Emanuel's insights about the characteristics and best practices of effective movement catalysts are profound and well-researched. I have found them timely and helpful in my own work of pursuing movements.

In 2007, I started a church called Experience Life in Lubbock, TX. It grew quickly, and we expanded to multiple campuses in several West Texas cities. The Lord allowed us to see thousands come to Christ and be baptized in the first ten years. Then, at our church's tenth anniversary, we cast vision to our congregation to move from a megachurch ministry approach to a multiplication approach. We had seen thousands reached but felt the Lord leading us to pray for millions. We believed that could only happen through a multiplicative approach like disciple-making movements. That began our journey to pursue movements in West Texas, and now around the world.

In this book, Emanuel builds on his previous work and provides a helpful "movement ministry manual" for those of us praying to see movements start in our areas. He writes not from theory but based on his research into 147 movements worldwide, and supported by his personal experience seeing a movement birthed in a remote region of Sudan.

He's not guessing at "what actually starts movements." He has gathered substantial data, with academically rigorous analysis, to back it up. I believe this research will prove beneficial to all of us on this journey. Emanuel identifies key correlating factors that promote an environment where movements can flourish. And we would do well to pay attention.

Imagine the value of sitting down with a movement catalyst and hearing them share about the factors that led to a movement. Now imagine if someone interviewed more than a hundred movements and organized the data into a highly accessible, highly digestible form. That's what you hold in your hands with this book.

Movement proponents too often major on the methods and minor on the characteristics of the men and women God uses to catalyze movements. But Emanuel's research shows we've got it totally backward. Methods matter, but people matter more. As Emanuel says, "The right kind of person is more important than the right methods." The good news in this book is that, in many ways, we can grow into the kind of person God can use to catalyze movements, if he so pleases.

We, in the church in North America, would do well to follow the examples set by our brothers and sisters in Christ around the world, whom God is using in extraordinary ways. They are willing to lead us by their good example if we'll allow them to. We don't want Jesus to rebuke us as he did the Pharisees by saying, "You have a fine way of rejecting the commandment of God in order to establish your tradition" (Mark 7:9). I pray the church in North America (and around the world) would have ears to "hear what the Spirit says to the churches" (Rev. 2:7).

And when we hear the Spirit, may we be quick to obey.

This book will help you know where to start.

THE STORY BEHIND THIS BOOK

Hello, I'm glad you opened this book. I wrote it for anyone committed to the Great Commission: practitioners, ministry leaders, and thought leaders. In it, you'll find a unique variety of actionable insights for ministry praxis, whether you are a church planter starting from scratch or you lead a church or ministry. The insights come from the broadest research into Christian movements ever conducted globally— empirical research carried out at a high academic level. These findings reveal practical steps you can take, wherever you are on your journey toward a movement.

Although I've never considered myself much of a writer, this book felt like an unstoppable force, compelling me to write it. English is my second language, so I approach writing with "a limp." Yet I had a deep-seated desire to share the findings in this book with those committed to the Great Commission.

Almost everywhere I travel, I encounter people wrestling with the questions, "What actually starts a movement? What methods should I use?" The answers vary widely, sometimes even contradicting each other. We could easily list a hundred factors that are said to contribute to a movement. Even thought leaders—those who have written about movements and teach and train on them—describe several dozen different factors they view as essential for movement breakthrough. For example, I recently participated in meetings with some of the world's best-known catalysts, and one catalyst presented the "irreducible minimum DNA" of movements. He described twenty items. In the same meeting, another leader shared on the same topic. He also described twenty characteristics of movements. However, his list had minimal overlap with the other.

A mist among thought leaders becomes a fog among practitioners. That's our current reality. I have trained thousands and mentored dozens of practitioners and have deep conversations with others wherever I go. Many practitioners—using the movement training they received—have implemented the "seven steps" or "eight elements" they learned; and though they may have seen some encouraging initial growth, they now struggle. Many wrestle to pinpoint the essential factors that actually boost movement breakthrough, and they find it hard to identify and overcome the factors that block a movement's progress. Since they struggle to *understand* what needs to be done, they inevitably struggle to *do* what needs to be done.

I wanted to clear the "mist"—to understand movements more deeply and go beyond the personal opinions and intuitive insights of individual "movement experts." What was needed was an empirical and rigorous examination of what actually starts movements. So, my team at the Bethany Research Institute decided to conduct in-depth research into movements. We researched 147 movements in twenty-one countries, among more than a hundred different people groups in all six mega-cultures of the world.

We worked hard as a team for almost two years, conducting surveys and interviews with effective catalytic leaders and other church-planting pioneers. We carried out complex statistical analyses and mulled over mountains of data. For each movement and its primary catalyst, we gathered at least 106 data points, totaling more than 32,000 data points for the entire study. We discussed our findings, formulated tentative insights, went back to the data and found more evidence, formulated new tentative insights, analyzed the data again, and so forth until we all agreed that the data presented itself with penetrating clarity.

Since completing the study, we have published its findings in journals such as *Missiology, Global Missiology, Mission Frontiers, Evangelical Missions Quarterly, Journal of the Evangelical Missiological Society,* as well as in *Christianity Today.* For the last year and a half I have been writing articles on The Movement Catalysts Blog.[1] The response has been positive from global Christian leaders and movement thought leaders. And the responses from practitioners— whether doing movement-oriented ministry in North American suburbs, remote villages of the Sahel, the Andes Mountains, a tiny island in Indonesia, or an Indian metropolis—have encouraged me that the findings are actionable and helpful to many. Feedback from practitioners and thought leaders has helped me understand what will likely be most relevant for you, the reader of this book. You now hold the result in your hand.

THE STORY BEHIND THE STORY: GOD CAN USE YOU TOO!

In case you have ever wondered, *Could God really use me to start a movement?*, I want to share with you my story in broad strokes. I've dealt personally with this question many times. Today, I still think, *If God could use me, he certainly can use anyone.*

When I decided to radically follow Jesus at the age of eighteen, I was a super-shy and inhibited young man. I had no confidence at all. In high school, when the teacher asked a question, I would instantly raise my hand to offer an answer, only to pull it back down again even more quickly. I knew I could likely give the right answer, but what if my answer wasn't 100 percent accurate? Worse, what if one of my classmates made a mocking comment that embarrassed me? So, arm down! Thinking about my future life for Jesus, I began to pray: "God, please use me. I have no idea how I will ever be of any use to you, but if you can make something out of my life, here I am. I am all yours."

I also began reading the Bible. Early on, in the Gospel of Matthew, I stumbled on Jesus' reference to "all peoples"—"And this gospel of the kingdom will be proclaimed throughout the whole world as a testimony to *all* nations, and then the end will come (Matt. 24:14, emphasis added). I soon found out that the Greek for "all nations"—*pasin tois ethnesin*[2]—*more accurately means "all peoples."* Jesus will not return without the gospel first going to *all peoples.* The same applies to the Great Commission: "Go therefore and make disciples of *all nations*" (Matt. 28:19, emphasis added). *All* peoples. *All!* Even as a naïve young Christian, I concluded: *We, the church, need to continue to make disciples where we are but make it our highest priority to make disciples among those peoples who still have zero disciples.* So my prayer became: "God, please send me to a people group that has zero disciples and use me to make disciples among them. And reveal to me how you want to use me."

Two years later, during my first semester in seminary, my mission professor devoted one lecture to what at that time was called "people movements." I was absolutely stunned. The idea of a people movement so intrigued me that I drove 100 kilometers to a university library containing every missiological book ever published in the English language. I borrowed every single book with the word "movement" in the title and photocopied every page. At the time, I found only a little over half a dozen titles. This was in the 1990s, before the concept of church-planting movements became popular. My prayer now became: "God, please use me to start a movement among the unengaged people group you will send me to; and reveal to me what you want to accomplish among them."

A couple of years later, God did reveal that. He showed me in a dream that he would start a massive movement to Christ among a 100-percent Muslim people group and that he would use me to catalyze it.

Ten years later, that dream became a reality. God used me to start a movement. In the middle of a civil war, in remote villages of Sudan, within a matter of days, hundreds of Muslims decided to become Jesus-followers. That number later multiplied to become many thousands. Today, the movement has spread across an entire region, with churches more than 200 kilometers from where it first broke out. I have already told that story on my blog and in podcasts.[3]

I prayed another bold prayer before we saw a movement: "God, please use me to start a movement among the unengaged people group you will send me to because your church and the missions community need that movement ministry paradigm. I can only contribute to bringing it to them if I speak with the credibility of my own experience." God answered that prayer. This book is part of his answer.

Soon after the movement emerged, my leaders asked me to mentor and train others. In my mentoring relationships, I always asked myself and the Father: "What does this person need most?" Despite having partnered with God to start a movement, I often wished for greater clarity about what essential factors contributed to catalyzing movements.

I also asked myself, *How can I help this person grow? What qualities are essential for him or her to develop?* Likewise, I often wished I knew the essential qualities of effective catalytic leaders. When I was first asked to create a movement training package, I had plenty of ideas of what to pack into the three-day training module. But I had only three days ... fifteen sessions at most. I wrestled: *What do these practitioners most need training in? What traits and competencies do they most need developed? What methods are essential for them to master, given the factors that contribute to catalyzing a movement?* How I wished for clearer answers!

This wrestling birthed in me the desire to conduct research that would find answers to my burning questions. In talking to other movement mentors, I heard them echo my wrestling. So, I carried out research into thirty-five movements in the Muslim world and found some answers.[4] The findings resulted in my book *Movement Catalysts*[5] and the *EXPONENTIAL Disciple-Making* training.[6]

The insights from that study have helped train over twelve thousand practitioners within a few years, with roughly two hundred more being trained every month. The workshops I have delivered for organizations and networks and the podcasts and webinars I've contributed to have been well received. But only God truly knows their impact.

David Garrison wrote in his foreword to *Movement Catalysts* that it "has shown us the way to better preparing God's people to become the kind of servant-leaders, movement catalysts, that He delights in using."[7]

Yet I wasn't content. I wanted to carry out similar research with a larger sample of effective catalytic leaders from across the globe in order to validate the findings more broadly. I also wanted to examine a control group of other pioneers who had not catalyzed a movement. This would give us answers to the question, "What distinguishes effective movement catalysts from non-catalysts?"

Together with my team at Bethany Research Institute, that study was realized. This book distills the study's most relevant insights.[8] I pray that you not only learn more about movements but, more importantly, that you gain a deeper awareness of how to partner with God in pursuing a movement.

HOW TO USE THIS BOOK

This book is designed as a practical "movement ministry manual," offering actionable steps to help you catalyze a movement. It's more than just research; it's a guide to personal and team development.

To help you navigate this journey, the book is divided into six sections: In part one, the movement landscape is introduced, providing essential context. Part two emphasizes the critical role of catalytic leaders and their personal attributes and identifies key qualities that can be developed to effectively catalyze movements. In part three, the six key elements most strongly correlated with movement breakthrough are unveiled. Each of these movement boosters is explored in detail. Part four explores two key factors that significantly hinder movement growth, along with strategies to address these blockers. In part five, you'll discover how to develop catalytic leadership skills through self-assessment and intentional growth. This section also offers a tool to analyze ministry contexts, to maximize movement-boosting factors, and mitigate those that block progress. Finally, part six addresses frequently asked questions about the interplay of divine sovereignty and human responsibility. This section also explores the role of miracles in catalyzing movements, offering both theological clarity and practical guidance.

Here's how to get the most out of the book.

Pray Before Reading: Every chapter begins with a prayer to help you connect with God before diving into the content. Before each chapter, take a moment to pause, pray, and connect with God. Release to him any distractions and ask for his guidance as you read. Remember: Movements are started by partnering with God.

Focus on Personal Growth: This book emphasizes the importance of personal development. Many of the chapters have pathways to growth, which contain simple concrete growth steps to move you closer to catalyzing a movement. Catalyzing a movement is ultimately in God's hands, but your focus should be on growing into the kind of person God can use. Embrace the journey of personal and spiritual development.

Maximize Your Takeaways: Each chapter concludes with a dedicated section to help you personalize and apply the material. I encourage you to take the time to reflect on your insights and takeaways from each chapter before beginning the next.

Use as a Resource for Your Training and Mentoring: You will maximize your own learning when processing it with and passing it on to others. The identified movement boosters and blockers provide a framework for curriculum development and mentoring conversations.

PART ONE

Setting the Stage for Movements

In the context of global Christianity, a movement can be defined as "a rapid indigenous multiplication of disciples making disciples and churches planting churches in multiple streams within a people group to the fourth generation and beyond."[1]

This section explores the remarkable spread of such movements worldwide, highlighting the significant growth and impact they have had on global Christianity. Although there has been a phenomenal increase in movement practitioners and ministries adopting a movemental approach, a critical gap remains in our understanding of what actually starts movements. This section emphasizes the pivotal role of movement catalysts and provides insights from comprehensive research that identifies the traits and competencies of effective catalytic leaders.

UNDERSTANDING THE MOVEMENT LANDSCAPE

We are in the midst of a "movement" movement.
Kevin Higgins

As you prayerfully engage with this chapter, you'll gain a deeper understanding of the following topics:

- *An explosion of movements:* Discover the phenomenal spread of movements worldwide.
- *Evolving movement discourse:* Explore the current trajectory of movement dialogue.
- *Conversation gaps:* Identify the overlooked areas within movement conversations.
- *Bridging the gaps:* Understand how the research underlying this book addresses these gaps.

Before you begin this chapter, I encourage you to put the book down and pray. This is not merely a spiritual platitude. I mean it. Movements are started by partnering with God. Therefore, you will benefit most from this book by reading it while listening to what God is saying to *you*. I invite you to pause for a minute and connect in your heart with the Father, releasing to him anything that may keep you from being fully present. You may use these words:

Father, please show me what in this chapter you want me to learn, so I can align with your ways and partner with you more fully. Amen.

THE PHENOMENAL SPREAD OF MOVEMENTS

God is advancing his kingdom through global movements in unprecedented ways. My personal working definition of a movement is "a rapid indigenous multiplication of disciples making disciples and churches planting churches in multiple streams within a people group to the fourth generation and beyond."[1] More Jesus-followers than ever before in history believe in the movement paradigm, are beginning to realize God could use them to contribute to a movement, and are aspiring to start a movement themselves.

This is wonderful in many ways:

- Global Christianity is undergoing a seismic shift toward a movement paradigm, and we are reaching a tipping point.[2]
- The number of movement practitioners is increasing.
- The number of ministries adopting a movemental approach is increasing.
- Many people have expectant faith that movements will happen.
- More and more movements are emerging as a result of the previous factors.

Figure 1.1 shows how movements are mushrooming around the globe. A graph says more than a thousand words, and figure 1.1 illustrates how significant the growth has been. As of 2024, researchers report 1,967 movements worldwide, with 115 million Jesus-followers. About 8.5 million new churches have been planted.[3] If accurate, this encompasses more than 1.4 percent of the entire population of the planet—about one in every seventy of all humans—and approximately 15 percent of all evangelical Christians globally. This translates to an annual growth rate in the number of disciples within movements of 23 percent, with numbers doubling every 3.5 years.

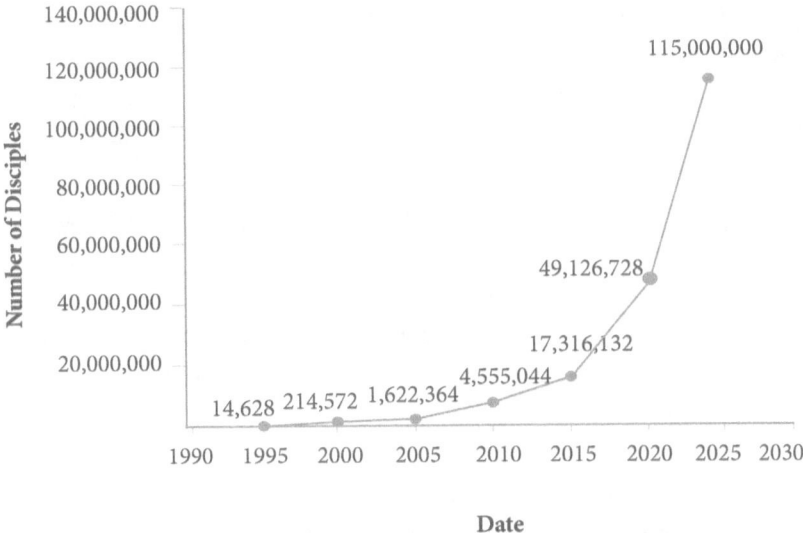

Figure 1.1: Increase in Disciples in Movements[4]

As such, the phenomenon of movements represents a critical mass,[5] with the numbers continuing to grow rapidly. This critical mass has the potential to reach a tipping point and significantly alter the trajectory of global Christianity, thus impacting the world. Nothing less than a seismic shift is happening right before our eyes. We stand at a potential turning point in history!

THE MOVEMENT DISCOURSE IN BROAD STROKES

Movements have become a key focus in global missions over the past decade.[6] These movements, despite varying conceptualizations, share the following elements:

- Rapid growth
- Multiplication of disciples
- Multiplication to at least a hundred churches or a thousand disciples
- Four or more generations of churches reproducing churches
- Multiple streams of churches

Researchers have examined a number of movements from across the globe, primarily in an attempt to identify elements that occur in the genesis of all or most of them. (See appendix one for a list of those elements by various authors.)

GAPS IN THE CONVERSATION: THE FACTORS THAT BOOST MOVEMENTS

Movement researchers and thought leaders share a common, if somewhat limited, understanding of the characteristics of movements. Thanks to their work, we now understand what movements look like in their idealized form.

However, the question of how to ignite widespread movement growth persists globally. At a local level, many movement practitioners, though inspired by great stories and successful models, struggle to initiate movements in practice.

I believe two critical factors are essential for both the global level and local movement development.

First, we need to understand *what actually starts movements*. Although many have a general understanding of movements, a clear understanding of the factors that catalyze them is lacking. Empirical data on which to base this understanding is also lacking: What factors boost movements or block them?

Second, we need to shift from focusing primarily on the *right methods in order to also consider the right kind of catalysts*. Over the past two decades, much discussion has centered on the *how* of movements but neglected the *who*.[7] This book explores the critical question: "What kind of person does God use to initiate movements?" The research underlying this book reveals that the most crucial factor in catalyzing a movement is the right individual, followed by the appropriate method. A sole reliance on formulas and methods, without the right person to apply them, can limit their effectiveness in addressing unique local challenges. Instead, we need to ask, "What kind of person does God use to start movements?"

Until recently, no serious research had been undertaken to identify the factors initiating movements. We can build on the work of other authors by extracting from their lists of movement characteristics (appendix one) those elements especially pertinent at the very early stages. We can consider these as factors that contribute to starting a movement. These include:

- Prayer
- Holistic ministry
- Persons of peace
- Contagious relationships
- Abundant evangelism

However, no hard empirical data exists that would verify most of these factors. Do they actually play the role they are purported to play? How significant is the contribution of each? Up until now, the movement conversation has remained largely silent on this topic.

Allow me to compare this with the world of organizations. Jim Collins's influential research has provided valuable insights for organizational leaders over the past thirty years. Collins began by researching the characteristics of great organizations, resulting in the bestseller *Built to Last*.[8] Many of Collins's readers aspired to build great organizations but expressed frustration that they didn't know which factors turned good organizations into great ones. Collins conducted the research organizational leaders needed, and seven years later he published *Good to Great*.[9] It sold more copies than *Built to Last*, reflecting even greater interest in knowing *how* to make the needed changes.

In the context of Christian movements, David Garrison's *Church Planting Movements* serves a role similar to *Built to Last* by detailing the characteristics of movements.[10] Others have added to his findings, but there has been a notable gap in research equivalent to *Good to Great* that identifies the specific factors contributing to the catalyzing of movements. This book aims to fill that gap by providing empirical data and practical insights into what actually starts movements, offering actionable steps similar to those found in *Good to Great* for organizations.

THE BROADEST-EVER RESEARCH ON CHRISTIAN MOVEMENTS

The research underlying this book is the broadest study of church-planting and disciple-making movements to have been conducted so far. The research team of four included an anthropologist and a statistician (both elite university research fellows), an administrator/editor, and myself (a movement practitioner, coach, and researcher).

The weight and reliability of our research data are derived from the following factors:

Breadth: We researched a total of 147 movements. This represented more than 15 percent of all movements known to exist at the time—a significant and representative sample size.

Depth: We gathered 106 data points for each movement and its primary catalyst. This totals more than 32,000 data points for the entire study.

Diversity and universality: We examined movements in twenty-nine different countries, among at least 122 different people groups, in all six mega-cultures of the world. Such diversity allows for conclusions across cultures.

Comparison with non-catalysts: In addition to researching movements and their primary catalysts, we compared their data with data from a control group of 160 non-catalysts in the same or similar settings. This control group study enabled us to identify what distinguishes effective catalysts from non-catalysts.

In-depth analysis: We analyzed the data of all 307 survey responses, both qualitatively and quantitatively, using advanced statistical operations.

A SNEAK PEEK

Let me give you a preview of what we found.

To date, the movement discourse has focused heavily on *methods* of catalyzing. This book is meant to change the conversation because, although our research verifies the importance of methodology, it also reveals that the right method does not result in a movement unless the right kind of leader employs it. Every time God starts a movement, he uses a catalytic team or network to do it. Although every member of the team contributes, every team has a leader who plays a key role in whether a movement is started or not.

My team surveyed the leaders of the teams behind 147 movements and found that every one of them exhibits twenty-one qualities that they share in common. And we found clear, consistent differences between a person who catalyzes a movement and a person who doesn't. This book will present those differences.

Personal qualities aren't the only differences between catalysts and non-catalysts, however. Catalytic leaders also *do certain things* that non-catalysts generally don't do or don't do as well as catalysts. Effective catalytic leaders much more often employ what they believe is the "right" ministry strategy. They don't all agree on what the right strategy is! Nevertheless, an overwhelming majority favors one strategy model above all others, and even those who haven't adopted it wholesale borrow many of its features.

The research also uncovered *factors outside a catalytic leader's control* that make catalyzing a movement easier or harder. Effective catalytic leaders navigate obstacles and leverage opportunities to drive movement growth, and this book will reveal how they do that.

Finally, as our research and that of others shows, a person isn't just born with or without the qualities of an effective catalytic leader. He or she can grow in these traits and competencies. In fact, that's exactly what effective catalytic leaders do. At the end of this book, I give data-driven guidance about how you can grow into the kind of leader God apparently uses to catalyze a movement. You will also find growth plans in many of the chapters. In sum, this book is written to help any reader become the kind of leader who leads a team that catalyzes a movement and to show the strategy and practices catalytic leaders use to get there.

Maximizing Your Chapter Takeaways

Recap

- Movements are spreading phenomenally around the world.
- We understand a lot about the characteristics of movements.
- We don't understand enough about the factors that start those movements.
- The research underlying this book addresses this gap and can help you identify the factors most essential to attend to in your ministry.

Reconnect

Pause for a minute, connect again in your heart with the Father, and pray: *Father, please show me how you want me to live out what I've learned in this chapter, so I can align with your ways and partner with you more fully. Amen.*

Record

- The key insights God has given me in this chapter are:

- The questions I have for deeper reflection are:

Realize

- I sense God nudging me to implement these key insights through the following action steps:
  - Action Step 1

  - Action Step 2

  - Action Step 3

PART TWO

The Kind of Person God Uses to Start Movements

This section discusses the crucial role of catalytic leaders in initiating movements, emphasizing the importance of their personal attributes.

Chapter two outlines how limited attention has been given to the person of the catalyst, though some movement authors have acknowledged their essential role. The chapter highlights that, although their leadership is crucial, effective catalysts are not lone rangers but team players who build and lead small teams. The chapter underscores that the catalyzing of a movement relies on the combined efforts of a complementary team and a catalytic leader.

With that foundation laid, chapter three explores the essential qualities of effective catalytic leaders and delves into the personal attributes that characterize these leaders and contribute to the catalyzing of movements. Drawing from extensive research, the chapter identifies twenty-one specific qualities that effective catalytic leaders possess and distinguish them from non-catalysts. The chapter also emphasizes that these qualities can be developed through intentional practice, offering a roadmap for aspiring leaders to develop and grow into the kind of person God uses to catalyze movements.

2

THE CRITICAL ROLE OF THE CATALYTIC LEADER

The world has yet to see what God can do with a man fully consecrated to Him. By God's help, I aim to be that man.

Dwight L. Moody

As you prayerfully engage with this chapter, you'll gain a deeper understanding of the following topics:

- *The literature discourse on catalysts until now:* Discover what other movement experts have written about effective catalytic leaders.
- *The role of the catalytic leader in teams:* Explore how teams are usually the first things that effective leaders catalyze.
- *The composition of catalytic teams:* Understand the makeup of the teams built by catalytic leaders and which giftings are essential to their fruitfulness.

Before you begin reading this chapter, I encourage you to put the book down, pause, and pray. Connect in your heart with the Father, releasing to him anything that may keep you from being fully present.

Father, please show me what in this chapter you want me to learn and how you want me to grow, so I can align with your ways and partner with you more fully. Amen.

THE MISSING PIECE: PERSONAL ATTRIBUTES OF CATALYTIC LEADERS

Every movement needs one or more catalytic leaders for it to get started. However, the prevailing discourse on movements has not talked about what those catalysts are like and what qualities characterize them. The late Steve Smith, movement catalyst and mentor, was the first to publish "a profile of a movement catalyst."[1] This article drew on his own experience as a catalyst and mentor to other catalysts around the world, as well as the wisdom of Bill Smith, who is considered by some as the father of movements. Steve Addison, in his treatise on movement leadership, lists characteristics of movement pioneers by gleaning both from the life of the apostle Peter and from his personal experience of mentoring catalysts globally.[2] Trevor Larsen lays out what he has observed in the national "apostolic agents" he has mentored for many years and who have catalyzed a number of movements in one Southeast Asian country.[3] Most recently, Gene Wilson, overseer of a global team of catalysts, has written about the role of movement catalysts, including a description of characteristics and qualities drawn from publications by other authors.[4]

My own previous work on the topic identified empirically the traits and competencies of effective catalytic leaders.[5] Wilson, in *Emerging Gospel Movements: The Role of Catalysts*, referred to this study and reported: "Emanuel Prinz has done the most comprehensive research to this date on the qualities of movement leaders."[6] David Greenlee, lead researcher at Operation Mobilization, quotes the research underlying the book you are now reading as "the most extensive" and "the best in-depth research on movement catalysts."[7]

While recognizing the importance of teams, the research underlying this book has mainly concentrated on the unique role of the catalytic leader. Therefore, this book primarily focuses on the effective catalytic leader rather than their teams.

CATALYSTS AND THEIR TEAMS

Effective movement catalysts are not lone rangers. (And even the fictional masked Lone Ranger relied on his sidekick, Tonto.[8]) Catalysts are team players and network builders. They are apostolic leaders. Therefore, the first thing they catalyze is usually a team and a network of individuals who share their vision for a movement. Then, together with their team and network, they catalyze a movement.

A catalytic team is a group of individuals who have covenanted together to catalyze a movement and who exhibit the catalytic qualities described in this book. In a previous study, I examined the realities of these catalytic teams.[9] I defined team members as individuals who are resident locally and regularly contribute to the team's efforts to catalyze a movement. That study revealed the following key insights about the teams led by effective catalysts:

- Most effective catalysts work with rather small teams. The majority comprise a total of no more than four team members, some even only one or two. About a third had an overall team of six to twelve, and only one-sixth had an overall team of thirteen or more.
- All catalytic teams were either led by a near-culture national or, if led by an expatriate, they had one (16 percent of all teams) or several (84 percent of all teams) nationals on them.

Interestingly, when talking with members about their movement's origins, they often readily identified a specific person as the movement starter. They pointed to an individual catalyst rather than the catalytic team.

That assessment fits with leadership theory and supports the conviction that leadership expert John Maxwell has popularized: "Everything rises and falls on leadership."[10] Applied to movement ministry, it means that the catalyst as apostolic leader typically attracts a team to their person and/or their vision and retains them by building a team where members thrive. The movement ministry rises primarily on the leadership of the catalyst.

At the same time, the fact that all effective catalysts work with teams points to the invaluable contributions team members make to the catalyzing of the movement. To be clear: A catalyst cannot start a movement alone. They need the complementary contributions of a team. A movement requires the combined capabilities of a team, coupled with a catalytic team leader possessing the qualities we will describe in the next chapter.

Some catalytic leaders describe the complementarity of their team in terms of the APEST model popularized by Alan Hirsch,[11] meaning that their teams comprise at least one apostle (A) (the catalyst themselves), prophets (P), evangelists (E), shepherds (S), and teachers (T). These functions may be filled by five different individuals; in some cases, one team member has strong gifting in more than one function and fills more than one. Even though many catalytic teams aspire to realize the APEST model, in reality, most are a work in progress. Other catalysts emphasize that all catalytic team members should possess both an apostolic calling and function. While they would likely acknowledge the presence of prophetic, evangelistic, shepherding, and teaching gifts on their teams, these are secondary to the apostolic in each core team member.

Maximizing Your Chapter Takeaways

Recap

- Previous publications have given limited attention to the personal attributes of effective catalytic leaders.
- Teams are usually the first things that effective leaders catalyze.
- Catalytic leaders build teams with a particular make-up—with certain giftings essential for their fruitfulness.

Reconnect

Pause for a minute, connect again in your heart with the Father, and pray: *Father, please show me how you want me to live out what I've learned in this chapter, so I can align with your ways and partner with you more fully. Amen.*

Record

- The key insights God has given me in this chapter are:

- The questions I have for deeper reflection are:

Realize

- I sense God nudging me to implement these key insights through the following action steps:
    - Action Step 1

    - Action Step 2

    - Action Step 3

3

THE QUALITIES OF CATALYTIC LEADERS

There is a kind of person the Lord of the Harvest looks
on with favor and uses to start a movement.

Bill Smith

As you prayerfully engage with this chapter, you'll gain a deeper understanding of the following topics:

- *Essential traits and competencies of effective leaders:* Discover that wherever there is a movement, you'll find a person with certain qualities.
- *Qualities of catalytic leadership:* Identify the twenty-one specific qualities that characterize effective catalytic leaders.
- *Qualities that drive movement catalyzing:* Explore how these qualities contribute significantly to initiating movements.
- *Your leadership potential:* Understand that all these qualities can be developed, and you too can grow in them.

Before you begin reading this chapter, I encourage you to put the book down, pause, and pray. Connect in your heart with the Father, releasing to him anything that may keep you from being fully present.

Father, please show me what in this chapter you want me to learn and how you want me to grow, so I can align with your ways and partner with you more fully. Amen.

TRAITS AND COMPETENCIES OF EFFECTIVE LEADERS

Effective catalytic leaders use a variety of movement ministry approaches, as we will see. While there is no single method that leads to a movement, all those God has used to initiate a movement manifest the same set of traits and competencies. So wherever you see a movement, you will find a catalytic leader with these characteristics. If we sat down in a coffee shop with an effective catalytic leader from rural Kenya, one from an American city, another from an Indian metropolis, and another from an Indonesian island, even allowing for individual personalities and cultural differences, we would find all four of them remarkably alike in their essential traits and competencies. So, when looking at what factors lead to movement breakthrough, we first need to examine the person of the catalyst.

The key question is: *What traits and competencies characterize pioneers who have been instrumental in catalyzing a movement—and distinguish them from those who have not?*

Digging Deeper Into the Research

To answer the above question, I first studied all the relevant literature on apostolic and movement leadership, as well as "secular" empirical leadership studies. As a team, we then gathered every publication we could find that detailed traits and competencies of effective leaders. We consulted fourteen works on apostolic and movement leadership and seventeen reviews synthesizing more than six hundred empirical studies of "secular" leadership. Put together, these thirty-one works gave us 228 traits and competencies. We narrowed the list by including in our research only traits and competencies mentioned in at least three of the works we consulted. That gave us twenty-four traits and competencies. We applied these twenty-four to effective movement catalysts to see which, if any, catalytic leaders consistently have, and which distinguished them from pioneers who had not started a movement.

We grouped these twenty-four into three domains, as follows (see table 3.1):

- The *Personality* domain: traits related to individual personality and character.
- The *Spiritual* domain: traits and competencies of a spiritual nature, having to do with one's relationship with God.
- The *Social Influence* domain: traits and competencies having to do with relating with others, describing social behavior and ways to influence others.

Table 3.1: Traits and Competencies Researched
with Effective Catalysts

Personality Traits	Spiritual Traits and Competencies	Social Influence Traits and Competencies
Radical Learning	Hunger for God	Extroversion
Innovation	Listening to God	Inspiring Personality
Drive to Achieve	Evangelistic Zeal	Influencing Others' Beliefs
Conscientiousness	Expectant Faith	Inspiring Shared Vision
Personal Agency	Deep Prayer	Assertiveness
Persistence	Tangible Love	Transformational Disciple-Making
Agreeableness	Confidence in Local Disciples	Empowering
Emotional Stability	Confidence in the Bible	
Flexibility		

THE TRAITS AND COMPETENCIES OF CATALYTIC LEADERS

Once we had identified the twenty-four qualities of effective leaders highlighted in movement and leadership literature, we surveyed effective movement catalysts, defined as those pioneers who

- have catalyzed a movement with churches that have multiplied to the fourth generation; and
- were the first to engage this people group with the gospel. They may not necessarily have been the first to ever share the gospel among the group but proved to be the most influential pioneer, even though others may have made significant contributions to launching the movement.

We also surveyed non-catalysts: pioneers serving in similar contexts who had not catalyzed a movement. Through this comparison, we identified not only the traits and competencies that characterize effective catalysts but also those that distinguish effective catalysts from non-catalysts. To illustrate, all catalytic leaders may share a love for Coca-Cola or competence in studying the Bible, but those traits do not explain their effectiveness in catalyzing a movement. The data from the control group of non-catalysts enabled us to identify the distinctive traits and competencies that separate *effective* catalytic leaders from other committed, yet *less fruitful*, pioneers.

For twenty-one of the twenty-four traits and competencies identified as characterizing effective leaders, on a scale of 1–5, the effective catalysts rated themselves higher than non-catalysts (see table 3.2 below). The table shows these sorted according to the self-rating by catalysts in descending order. (You can find a definition of each of these attributes in table 3.5, at the end of this chapter.)

Table 3.2: Traits and Competencies Sorted by Self-Rating

Trait or Competency	Catalysts	Non-Catalysts	Difference
Confidence in Local Disciples	+4.88	+4.53	+0.35
Confidence in the Bible	+4.77	+4.39	+0.38
Assertiveness	+4.77	+4.29	+0.48
Influencing Others' Beliefs	+4.70	+4.19	+0.51
Conscientiousness	+4.69	+4.41	+0.28
Tangible Love	+4.69	+4.43	+0.26

Trait or Competency	Catalysts	Non-Catalysts	Difference
Evangelistic Zeal	+4.68	+4.39	+0.29
Expectant Faith	+4.67	+4.36	+0.31
Inspiring Shared Vision	+4.66	+4.23	+0.43
Transformational Disciple-Making	+4.65	+4.07	+0.58
Empowering	+4.63	+4.11	+0.52
Agreeableness	+4.60	+4.16	+0.44
Inspiring Personality	+4.60	+4.06	+0.54
Hunger for God	+4.51	+4.15	+0.36
Listening to God	+4.51	+4.16	+0.35
Radical Learning	+4.44	+4.19	+0.25
Personal Agency	+4.43	+4.11	+0.32
Drive to Achieve	+4.41	+4.14	+0.27
Innovation	+4.32	+3.86	+0.46
Persistence	+4.30	+3.98	+0.32
Deep Prayer	+3.83	+3.07	+0.76

Table 3.3 below shows the difference in ratings between the catalysts and non-catalysts, sorted in order of greatest significance.

Table 3.3: Difference between Ratings by Catalysts and Non-Catalysts

Significant (difference of 0.25–0.50 Likert point)	Highly significant (difference of more than 0.50 Likert point)
Assertiveness (+0.48)	Deep Prayer (+0.76)
Innovation (+0.46)	Transformational Disciple-Making (+0.58)
Agreeableness (+0.44)	Inspiring Personality (+0.54)
Inspiring Shared Vision (+0.43)	Empowering (+0.52)
Confidence in the Bible (+0.38)	Influencing Others' Beliefs (+0.51)
Confidence in Local Disciples (+0.35)	
Listening to God (+0.35)	
Hunger for God (+0.36)	

Significant (difference of 0.25–0.50 Likert point)	Highly significant (difference of more than 0.50 Likert point)
Personal Agency (+0.32)	
Persistence (+0.32)	
Expectant Faith (+0.31)	
Conscientiousness (+0.28)	
Evangelistic Zeal (+0.29)	
Drive to Achieve (+0.27)	
Tangible Love (+0.26)	
Radical Learning (+0.25)	

Digging Deeper Into the Research: Similarity of Same-Culture, Near-Culture and Expatriate Catalysts

Questions have arisen about the roles and functions of expatriate catalysts versus near-culture catalysts and same-culture catalysts. The data demonstrates minimal differences between the traits and competencies of these groups as related to movements, as illustrated by table 3.4 below. The table shows the traits and competencies distinguished by the origin of the main catalyst, whether an expatriate, a member of a neighboring people group in the same country (near-culture), or a member of the same people group (same-culture). The table only includes the five traits and competencies that exhibit a statistically significant difference between these three groups.

Table 3.4: Rating of Traits and Competencies Compared by Origin of Main Catalyst

Traits and Competencies	Average	Variation		
		Expatriate	Near Culture	Same Culture
Agreeableness	4.36	-0.12	-0.21	+0.11
Deep Prayer	3.41	-0.5	-0.15	+0.13
Inspiring Personality	4.32	-0.26	+0.06	+0.05

Traits and Competencies	Average	Variation		
		Expatriate	Near Culture	Same Culture
Influencing Beliefs	4.43	–0.15	–0.18	+0.1
Transformational Disciple-Making	4.34	–0.28	+0.07	+0.07

Given that only five of the twenty-four traits and competencies assessed showed a statistically significant divergence between the three groups, and even those differences are minimal, we conclude that catalytic leaders from different cultural backgrounds have far more similarities than differences. The data shows no support for a differentiation between catalysts' place of origin when it comes to their unique function or their ability to catalyze a movement. The origin of the catalytic leader influences their effectiveness in catalyzing a movement but does not determine it. Movements may be catalyzed by expatriates too, despite their disadvantages of being outsiders culturally, as long as they enculturate well and exhibit the qualities of a catalytic leader.

SUMMARY AND CONCLUSIONS

Our research identified twenty-one traits and competencies that characterize effective catalytic leaders and positively distinguish them from leaders who have not catalyzed movements. Wherever in the world a movement has been catalyzed, God has used a catalytic leader who consistently exhibits this combination of characteristics.

This insight should jolt missions thinkers to shift emphasis from the "right" ministry methods toward greater emphasis on the "right" person. To be more precise, we need to move from the most suitable *ministry methods* to the most suitable *person*—and how such a person can be developed and trained. Reflecting on the traits and competencies of those God uses to catalyze a movement can help identify areas for improvement and growth and can offer a roadmap for personal and spiritual growth. Mission educators, trainers, and mentors need to ensure that their formulation of fruitful methods is wedded to the formation of the needed traits and competencies identified by the research. The list of traits and competencies presented in this chapter gives mission trainers a blueprint for training curricula and points mentors to areas on which to build. By focusing on these traits and competencies in trainees and mentees, they can more effectively develop fruitful catalytic leaders for the kingdom.

These findings also encourage leaders hoping to catalyze a movement to focus on developing positive traits and competencies within themselves and their teams rather than being concerned about external factors beyond their control, such as a lack of openness to the gospel or local opposition. All the traits and competencies presented in this book can be developed through intentional and deliberate practice—some to a limited degree but most very significantly. This proactive approach will be far more likely to lead to fruitful movement outcomes.

To catalyze a movement ultimately lies outside the immediate influence of any of us to achieve. Our personal growth, however, is primarily within our control and responsibility. With this encouragement, let all of us who aspire to start a movement grow into the kind of person God is pleased to use! (Chapter sixteen will give you a practical journey map for how to do this.)

Maximizing Your Chapter Takeaways

Recap

- Wherever you see a movement, you'll find a person with certain qualities.
- Twenty-one qualities characterize effective catalytic leaders.
- These qualities contribute significantly to movement catalyzing.
- All these qualities can be developed, and you too can grow in them.

Reconnect

Pause for a minute, connect again in your heart with the Father, and pray: *Father, please show me how you want me to live out what I've learned in this chapter, so I can align with your ways and partner with you more fully. Amen.*

Record

- The key insights God has given me in this chapter are:

Reflect More Deeply

Use the following self-coaching questions for prayerful personal or team reflection:

- Which of the twenty-one qualities that characterize effective catalytic leaders fit the profile of the catalysts I have known who have started a movement?
- How does this perspective—that the catalytic leader's qualities contribute significantly to movement catalyzing—fit into my ministry philosophy?
- When I look at the list of twenty-one qualities, what is my reaction? Do I feel a positive challenge to want to grow into such a person? Or do I feel discouraged by the gap between my current state and that list of qualities?
- How do I feel about the perspective that all these qualities can be developed?
- When contemplating the catalytic qualities, which of the twenty-one do I feel particularly motivated to develop more in my life?

Realize

- I sense God nudging me to implement these key insights through the following action steps:
  - Action Step 1

  - Action Step 2

  - Action Step 3

Table 3.5: Definitions of Traits and Competencies of
Effective Catalytic Leaders

Personality Traits	Spiritual Traits and Competencies	Social Influence Traits and Competencies
Radical Learning: Effective catalytic leaders maintain a posture of actively engaging in experiences in an open-minded way, expecting they will find something new to learn.	**Hunger for God:** Effective catalytic leaders desire depth in their relationship with God and yearn to know and love him more deeply, evidenced by extended and habitual practice of spiritual disciplines chosen for best fit.	**Inspiring Personality:** Effective catalytic leaders display a sense of authority and confidence, acting selflessly in ways that build other people's respect for them and instilling a sense of honor in others for being associated with them.
Innovation: Effective catalytic leaders use their imagination to come up with new and original ideas and innovative approaches.	**Listening to God:** In a posture of dependence on God, effective catalytic leaders regularly take time to listen to him—waiting on him, seeking guidance for life and ministry, and being obedient to whatever he says.	**Influencing Others' Beliefs:** Effective catalytic leaders talk often about their most important values and beliefs, considering the moral consequences of decisions with people and emphasizing the importance of living toward a purpose.
Drive to Achieve: Effective catalytic leaders are motivated to achieve goals, get things done, and attain results; they focus effort on decisive actions.	**Evangelistic Zeal:** Effective catalytic leaders are driven by a passionate urgency to see the good news shared with all the lost; they passionately share the good news with everyone possible.	**Inspiring Shared Vision:** Effective catalytic leaders articulate a compelling vision of the future, talking enthusiastically about what needs to be accomplished and expressing confidence that goals will be achieved.

Personality Traits	Spiritual Traits and Competencies	Social Influence Traits and Competencies
Conscientiousness: Effective catalytic leaders have a tendency to display self-discipline, act dutifully, and strive for achievement against measures or outside expectations, related to the way in which they control, regulate, and direct their impulses.	**Expectant Faith:** Effective catalytic leaders exercise faith that God will show his power through their lives, in particular, expectant faith that God will grow a movement and save many.	**Assertiveness:** Effective catalytic leaders are motivated to influence people and situations, even to the extent of dominating; sharing their beliefs and convictions clearly so that people take notice and being bold and courageous even when facing opposition and threat.
Personal Agency: Effective catalytic leaders believe they have control over the outcome of the events in their lives—as opposed to external forces beyond their influence—and that life outcomes derive primarily from their own actions.	**Deep Prayer:** Effective catalytic leaders pray regularly for extended times on behalf of their adopted people—for many to be saved in a growing movement.	**Transformational Disciple-Making:** Effective catalytic leaders do intentional Bible-centered teaching in the context of a transformational relationship that leads to heart obedience, encompassing spiritual disciplines and character formation.
Persistence: Effective catalytic leaders have the capacity to work with distant goals in view, to be tenacious in spite of challenges, and to overcome obstacles and not give up amidst difficulties.	**Tangible Love:** Effective catalytic leaders take a genuine interest in the lives and welfare of the people they reach out to, caring for them and expressing love to them in tangible ways.	**Empowering:** Effective catalytic leaders recognize the gifts of others, enabling them to develop these gifts, assigning responsibility and authority to others—including relinquishing control and risking failure, and equipping others to carry out assigned responsibilities by means of mentoring, coaching, or training.

Personality Traits	Spiritual Traits and Competencies	Social Influence Traits and Competencies
Agreeableness: Effective catalytic leaders have a concern for social harmony that motivates them to seek out and maintain close social relationships; to be considerate, kind, generous, trusting, trustworthy, helpful, characterized by pleasant companionship, and willing to compromise their own interests when interacting with others.	**Confidence in Local Disciples:** Effective catalytic leaders are confident that God—by the efficacy of his Word and Spirit—can grow and use new and immature believers and hence grow a local movement from local resources.	
	Confidence in the Bible: Effective catalytic leaders are confident that God's Word contains eternal principles, making it the ministry guidebook and foundational discipleship tool, hence a key ingredient in the growth of even the youngest disciples.	

PART THREE

Movement Boosters

In the next chapters we will focus on the six most critical elements positively corelated with movement breakthrough. Three of these elements are *leader qualities* and three are *ministry factors*. We will refer to these six elements as *correlating movement boosters*. Understanding a correlation will help you see the weight of these six elements. A correlation is a "connection or relationship between two or more facts."[1] It means that where you see one phenomenon, you will find the other too; and one phenomenon influences, or may cause, the other. Scientifically proven statistical operations can determine correlations between two phenomena—in our case between a movement and a certain element boosting the movement.

While we will focus primarily on the three correlating qualities in this part of the book, our study examined twenty-one *qualities* of the catalysts. (You can see the whole list in chapter three.) In addition, from among the many ministry *factors* that have been mentioned as boosting or blocking a movement,[2] our study examined twenty-one. (See chapter ten for a list of all the boosting factors and chapter fourteen for the blocking factors.)

To give you an idea of the rigor in our study, note that, for each movement and its primary catalyst, we gathered more than 106 data points. This totals more than 32,000 data points for the entire study.

(For more on the data points, see appendix two.) Through statistical analysis of our representative sample of 147 movements worldwide, our research revealed that, out of the forty-two combined elements, just three leader *qualities* and three *factors* most directly correlate with boosting movements.

LEADER *QUALITIES* THAT POSITIVELY CORRELATE WITH MOVEMENT BREAKTHROUGH

Among the *qualities* of a catalytic leader, the following show a *direct correlation* with movement breakthrough:

- Deep Prayer
- Influencing Others' Beliefs
- Assertiveness

We compared effective catalytic leaders with other pioneers in the same context who had not catalyzed a movement. Both groups were asked the same set of questions related to each catalytic quality, and they were also directed to assess themselves on a scale from 1 ("definitely doesn't apply to me") to 5 ("definitely applies to me"). Table III.1 presents how highly these leaders assessed their catalytic qualities, and the clear difference between effective catalysts and non-catalysts.

Table III.1: Catalysts' Qualities Correlating
with Movement Breakthrough

Catalytic Quality	Catalysts	Non-Catalysts	Difference
Deep Prayer	3.83	3.07	+0.76
Influencing Others' Beliefs	4.70	4.19	+0.51
Assertiveness	4.77	4.29	+0.48

MINISTRY *FACTORS* THAT POSITIVELY CORRELATE WITH MOVEMENT

Of the twenty-one *factors* identified as boosting or blocking a movement, the three that correlated positively with the catalyzing of movements are all *internal* factors—ministry approaches that catalytic leaders put into place together with their teams and partners. These three factors are:

- Developing an effective ministry strategy
- Using a discovery approach and discovery groups
- Effectively raising up leaders

In our research, we asked both catalysts and non-catalysts how much each factor contributed to the catalyzing of their movement. Table III.2 shows how highly they rate the three factors correlating positively with movement breakthrough. The table also shows a clear difference between effective catalysts and non-catalysts.

Table III.2: The Factors Correlating with Movement Breakthrough

Factors	Catalysts	Non-Catalysts	Difference
Developed Effective Ministry Strategy	4.51	3.71	+0.80
Used Discovery Approach/ Groups	4.16	3.45	+0.72
Effectively Raised Up Leaders	4.55	3.75	+0.81

In this section, chapters four through six examine the top three *leader qualities,* and chapters seven through nine explore the top three *ministry factors* that directly correlate with movement growth. Chapter ten looks at other factors mentioned most frequently by practitioners as contributing to or boosting movements. Chapter eleven summarizes the findings by examining how the combination of the right person and the right methods initiate movements.

4

Correlating Movement Booster #1

LEADER QUALITY: DEEP PRAYER

*The prevailing notion is that sheer volume—"much prayer"—
is the key to movemental breakthrough. Instead [it is] "deep
prayer"—a prayer life marked by intimacy with God, attentiveness
to his voice, and a profound alignment with his purposes.*

Alan Hirsch

As you prayerfully engage with this chapter, you'll gain a deeper
understanding of the following topics:

- *"Much prayer"*: Discover that not all catalytic leaders have "much
  prayer" in common.
- *"Deep prayer"*: Understand that catalytic leaders all engage in
  "deep prayer," which correlates with movement breakthrough.
- *Grow in prayer*: Learn and identify practical steps you can take
  to deepen your prayer life.

Before you begin reading this chapter, I encourage you to put the book
down, pause, and pray. Connect in your heart with the Father, releasing
to him anything that may keep you from being fully present.

Father, please show me what in this chapter you want me to learn and how you want me to grow, so I can align with your ways and partner with you more fully. Amen.

HOW MUCH DO CATALYTIC LEADERS PRAY?

You may have heard it said: "Two hours or more of daily prayer is standard among movement catalysts." We wanted to find out if this was an urban legend or actually held true. So we asked effective catalytic leaders to tell us how many hours on average they spend praying each week—by themselves or with others—on behalf of their adopted people.

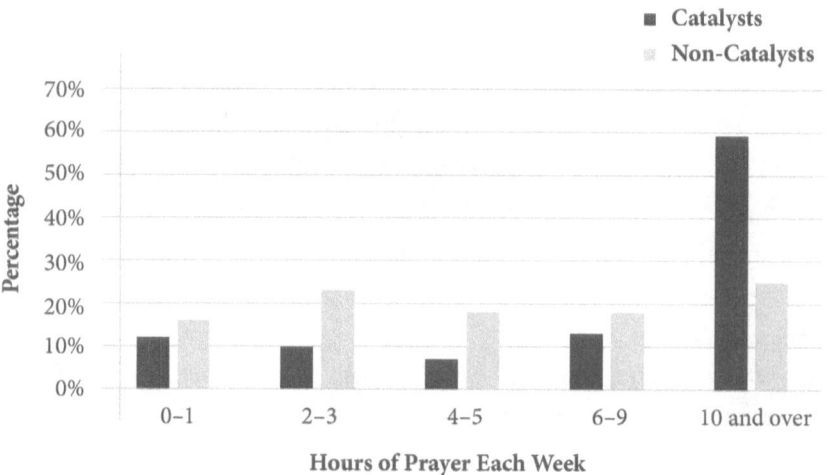

Figure 4.1: Hours of Prayer for Catalysts versus Non-Catalysts

You can see that 41 percent of all effective catalytic leaders report they pray on behalf of their adopted people less than ten hours each week. This translates to less than one and a half hours each day. So, the claim about effective catalysts' prayer lives was not confirmed. However, 59 percent of them do spend ten or more hours in prayer every week. Of all catalytic leaders, 7 percent pray four to five hours every week (less than one hour daily) on behalf of their adopted people, 10 percent pray two to three hours weekly (less than half an hour daily), and 12 percent pray for this zero to one hour weekly (under ten minutes daily).

When we compare the hours effective catalysts spend in prayer with the hours of non-catalysts, we see a massive difference. Whereas 59 percent of all effective catalysts spend ten hours or more in prayer for their adopted people each week, only 25 percent of non-catalysts do.

Several insights stand out:

- Most effective movement catalysts pray a lot.
- Many effective movement catalysts pray more than other pioneers who have not started a movement.
- A good portion (41 percent) of effective catalysts pray significantly less than has been assumed.
- Some effective catalysts don't spend much time in prayer on behalf of their adopted people group (less than thirty minutes a day or even less than ten minutes a day).

Thus, the correlation between being a powerful intercessor and the ability to catalyze a movement is not based solely on the amount of time spent in prayer.

Ultimately, the data does not support the hypothesis that the amount of time praying is a significant factor in a catalytic leader's ability to catalyze a movement. Some catalytic leaders pray surprisingly little, yet they have started a movement. Is there another correlation? In other words, is there something about their prayer that influences movement outcomes?

I had a hunch that if it isn't the *quantity* of prayer, it must be the *quality*; but as a team we wanted to counter any confirmation bias and let the data speak for itself. So we investigated further. Our working hypothesis was that the *depth* of effective movement catalysts' prayer life, rather than its *length*, is the primary determinant of its influence. Therefore we went back to the data to find out which attributes characterized catalysts' prayer lives. We wanted to answer the question: *How deeply do effective catalysts pray?* Aware of potential confirmation bias, we did find that their prayer lives are marked by a certain quality or depth.

MARKS OF THE DEEP PRAYER OF CATALYTIC LEADERS

Catalytic leaders consistently reported their prayer lives exhibited the following qualities:

- Their deepest desire is **hunger for God**. They yearn to know and love him more deeply. They long for God himself and for genuine relationship with him, more deeply than they desire a movement. They don't seek God primarily in order for him to give them something—a movement—which would be using God as a means for an end. Rather, God himself is the end they seek.
- Their posture is **listening to God**. They regularly take time to hear from him, wait on him, and seek guidance for their life and ministry, ready to obey whatever he says.
- Their prayer is fueled by **expectant faith** that God will show his power through their lives and will grow a movement and bring many to saving faith.
- The world-oriented outflow is **fervent intercession**. Catalytic leaders pray regularly and passionately on behalf of their adopted people—for many to be saved in a growing movement.

These four qualities mark the prayer lives of catalytic leaders. Although the amount of time they pray for their people group varies considerably—from more than one and a half hours per day down to less than ten minutes a day—they show consistency in the qualities of their prayer.

A CASE AGAINST AN OVER-EMPHASIS ON MUCH PRAYER

The depth that marks the prayer life of catalytic leaders contrasts with a common misconception among many Christians. A local church I attended once experienced an unusually high turnout at their weekly prayer meeting. The leader expressed excitement, suggesting that the increased number or people would increase the likelihood of prayers being answered. Have you ever heard a similar sentiment? This is magical thinking! This belief, rooted in folk religion, is prevalent in Christian circles and affects the way many Christians think about what great prayer looks like. We must reject the notion that more prayers equates to more answered prayers, even though it may be widely accepted.

Recently, I had an interesting conversation with a Buddhist taxi driver in Singapore. In his taxi, he had a mani prayer wheel, a device containing mantras and prayers. Buddhists believe that spinning the wheel, which symbolizes the recitation of these prayers, will earn them more spiritual merit. Ironically, technological development has led to electric-powered prayer wheels that can spin continuously and at greater speed. We may view such prayer practices with skepticism, but the belief that God is more likely to answer more frequent and longer prayers is equally misguided.

Consider this instruction of our Master: "When you pray, do not use a lot of meaningless words, as the pagans do, who think that their gods will hear them because their prayers are long" (Matt. 6:7 GNT). Jesus himself denounces such belief as pagan. He offers a kingdom alternative: "Do not be like them. Your Father already knows what you need before you ask him" (Matt. 6:8 GNT). In essence, when we pray to a caring Abba Father, neither the number of words nor the length of our prayers matters. What does matter is knowing our Father, who knows what we need. The quality of our relationship with our Father makes all the difference. And that quality marks the prayer life of catalytic leaders.

HOW DO MUCH PRAYER AND DEEP PRAYER RELATE?

To avoid any misunderstanding, it's important to note that Jesus doesn't oppose much prayer (and nor do I). Human relationships offer a helpful analogy to help us understand how *much prayer* integrates with *deep prayer*. In marriage or friendship, the more two people talk with each other, the longer their history, the more experiences they share, the deeper the relationship can become. However this does not happen automatically. Quantity alone does not guarantee quality. We've all experienced great hopes for friendships that, despite frequent interaction, never truly deepened, and eventually fizzled out. A certain level of interaction is necessary, though, to develop depth.

At the same time, we can go very deep with others in very little time. I recently had a profound eighty-minute Zoom conversation with a well-known global church leader whom I had never met before. We shared our hearts authentically and vulnerably, resulting in a deeply meaningful encounter.

Catalytic leaders have developed deep prayer—marked by hunger for God himself, a posture of listening to God, filled with expectant faith, and flowing out in fervent intercession. Deep prayer frequently leads to much prayer, and much prayer in turn deepens prayer further. The spiral continues to go deeper and deeper.

Figure 4.2: The Spiral of Deep Prayer in Catalysts' Lives

From Experience: A Deepening Prayer Life

I am reluctant to describe my prayer life as deep. Rather, I tend to see aspects of my prayer life where I long to experience much more of God's reality and get to know him more deeply. I can say that my prayer life has been "deepening." In my *hunger for God*, I have sought him for revelation for my life. And God has spoken. Once, after I asked him specifically to speak, he gave me a dream the following night. In that dream he showed me that his plan was to write church history in the part of Sudan to which I felt called. At that time (1997), there were less than a handful of believers among the thirty-five different people groups and more than seven million people of that region. *Listening to God* through the dream birthed in me the *expectant faith* that one day I would see a movement grow. That expectant faith fueled my *fervent intercession* to pray that dream into being, until—eight years after I had the dream—the breakthrough happened.

A GROWTH PATH TO DEEPER PRAYER

To grow *in deep prayer*, you can take some specific steps gleaned from the lives of catalytic leaders.

- Plan time for deep prayer and intercession into your weekly schedule, as you would for any other important activity.
- Deep prayer is more caught than taught. Pray together with others whose prayer life is deeper than your own.
- Study and pray the prayers of the Bible.
- Be on the lookout for "small beginnings" as answers to your prayers and let them build up your faith. I journal daily on the question, "Where have I seen God's hand in my day?"
- Record anything God has spoken to you that you can build your expectant faith on; anything about your calling, your team's calling, and anything about God's vision for your people and what he wants to do among them. This can be through Scripture, prophetic words, dreams, visions, or impressions.
- Use what God has spoken as the fuel for your prayers and as promises you pray into being.

Maximizing Your Chapter Takeaways

Recap

- Not all catalytic leaders have "much prayer" in common.
- Catalytic leaders do have "deep prayer" in common, which correlates with movement breakthrough.
- Deep prayer is marked by *hunger for God*, a posture of *listening to God*, and being filled with *expectant faith*—all of which flow out in *fervent intercession*.

Reconnect

- Pause for a minute, connect again in your heart with the Father, and pray: *Father, please show me how you want me to live out what I've learned in this chapter, so I can align with your ways and partner with you more fully. Amen.*

Record

- The key insights God has given me in this chapter are:

Reflect More Deeply

If you want to cultivate more depth in your prayer, I invite you to reflect on the current quality of your prayer life. Simply come into the Father's gracious presence and reflect on these self-coaching questions, which can be used for prayerful personal or team reflection:

- How deep is my hunger for God himself—my desire to feel close to him rather than asking him to do things (including growing a movement)?
- How much is my prayer posture one of dependence on God?
- How often and how well do I listen to God, rather than telling him things?
- What level of expectant faith do I have when I pray?
- How clearly has God spoken to me about what he intends to do through my ministry and in my people group? How do I want to seek him to receive more revelation?

Realize

- I sense God nudging me to implement these key insights through the following action steps:
  - Action Step 1

  - Action Step 2

  - Action Step 3

5

Correlating Movement Booster #2

LEADER QUALITY: INFLUENCING OTHERS' BELIEFS

[Paul] tried to persuade them about Jesus....
Some were convinced by what he said.
Acts 28:23–24 NIV, emphasis added

As you prayerfully engage with this chapter, you'll gain a deeper understanding of the following topics:

- *Influencing others' beliefs as a keystone factor:* Discover what it means to influence others' beliefs and why no other behavior of catalytic leaders correlates more strongly with movement breakthrough.
- *Biblical examples of influencing others' beliefs:* Learn how the apostle Paul brought people to conversion.
- *Best practices:* Explore the practical ways catalytic leaders influence others' beliefs.
- *Growing in influencing others' beliefs:* Learn and identify steps you can take to grow in this ability.

Before you begin reading this chapter, I encourage you to put the book down, pause, and pray. Connect in your heart with the Father, releasing to him anything that may keep you from being fully present.

Father, please show me what in this chapter you want me to learn and how you want me to grow, so I can align with your ways and partner with you more fully. Amen.

CHANGING THE MINDS OF OTHERS

"Oh, I wish I could change their mind!" Who has not had that desire at some point? Maybe it was with an individual or group outside the kingdom, held back from moving toward Christ by certain beliefs. Maybe it was with someone you fellowship with, who stubbornly clings to beliefs that hinder their growth. I have certainly felt that desire many times. I've tried to bring change, only to find it impossible to alter others' beliefs. However, influencing them *is* possible. Effective catalytic leaders have this ability.

From Experience: Influencing the Beliefs of Fifty Muslim Sheikhs

A watershed moment in the movement started by the team in Sudan I was leading provides a powerful illustration of influencing beliefs. Underneath a large Saharan tree, escaping the blazing sun, I sat in a circle with about fifty Muslim sheikhs—the chiefs of an entire region. We had embarked on a journey together considering the lives of three great prophets: Ibrahim, Musa, and Dawud (Abraham, Moses, and David). As we delved into the prophets' stories, we uncovered their flaws: Ibrahim's deceit, not trusting God; Musa's anger as he struck the rock, not trusting God; and Dawud's adultery and murder, disobeying God.

After each narrative, I asked the same questions: "Did this prophet sin? Did he need forgiveness?" On this day, the stories were about to reach their culmination. I posed the big question: "Did all these prophets reach God based on their merits?" A resounding "no" filled the air. When asked if the prophets needed God's grace to save them, all affirmed "yes."

I then asked them: "Have you found peace in your hearts striving to reach God based on your merits?" A heavy silence fell. I pressed further: "So, if these great men of God did not reach God based on their own merits, do you think we—any of us—stand a chance?" More silence followed, as the wheels in their minds turned. Deeply held paradigms were being influenced, undermined, shifted, changed. Conviction filled the space under the tree. Then one sheik, his voice heavy with sorrow, rumbled: "No. Not even close." The same "no" quietly escaped the mouths of others too, as they shook their heads and silently acknowledged the truth.

If you have ever worked with Muslims, you will know that they believe prophets are sinless and have earned God's favor through their merits.

Muslims believe that *they themselves* can earn God's favor through their merits. The beliefs of this group were significantly influenced and radically changed that day. Only someone who was once a Muslim can fully grasp how massive this change is. Suddenly they became open to the message of a Savior.

This example illustrates some of the key practices of *influencing others' beliefs*:

- Stories are told.
- Questions are asked.
- Dialog happens.
- The consequences of beliefs and lifestyles are considered.

WHAT DOES "INFLUENCING OTHERS' BELIEFS" MEAN?

To understand the nature of influencing others' beliefs, look at figure 5.1, a spectrum where the right end has "changing others' beliefs"—which is not realistic, as only the person holding their beliefs can change them—and the left end has merely "sharing our own beliefs"—which is insufficient if we want to influence others.

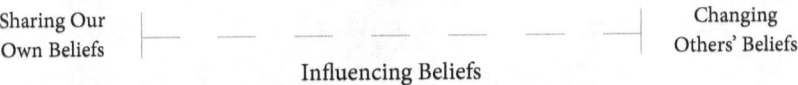

Sharing Our Own Beliefs

Influencing Beliefs

Changing Others' Beliefs

Figure 5.1: Influencing Beliefs Situated

In our research, we defined influencing others' beliefs as talking often about one's most important values and beliefs, considering the moral consequences of decisions with people, and emphasizing the importance of living toward a purpose.

As defined by Bernard Bass and Ronald Riggio in *Transformational Leadership*, a key text within the most influential stream of modern leadership thought, this competency is called "idealized influence."[1] Empirical research identified it as one of only four competencies of transformational leaders globally.[2] We should not be surprised that catalytic leaders exhibit it. From a movement-philosophy standpoint, the effective transference of spiritual beliefs and values lies at the core of movements. When this happens, it leads to the replication of disciples and churches.

INFLUENCING OTHERS' BELIEFS IN THE BOOK OF ACTS

Consider the following three verses from the book of Acts that describe the significant contribution to conversion ascribed to the movement catalyst Paul, as he influenced others' beliefs (emphasis added):

- "And you see and hear how this fellow Paul *has convinced* and led astray large numbers of people here in Ephesus and in practically the whole province of Asia. He says that gods made by human hands are no gods at all" (Acts 19:26 NIV).
- "I am sending you to them [the nations] to *open their eyes* and *turn them* from darkness to light, and from the power of Satan to God" (Acts 26:17–18 NIV).
- "[Paul] witnessed to them from morning till evening, explaining about the kingdom of God, and from the Law of Moses and from the Prophets he tried to *persuade* them about Jesus. Some were *convinced* by what he said, but others would not believe" (Acts 28:23–24 NIV).

The verbs used to describe conversions are all active: *open eyes, turn them, convince, persuade*. This conveys that convictions and persuasions were influenced by Paul's actions; people saw what they had not seen before ("eyes opened") and turned to God. The way Paul influenced others' beliefs clearly involved much more than friendship evangelism and sharing his testimony.

BEST PRACTICES FOR INFLUENCING OTHERS' BELIEFS

Catalytic leaders reported that they have incorporated the following practices into their lives and assess them to have boosted a movement.

Best Practice #1: Address the "destiny question." Every human being, regardless of their belief system, craves meaning, significance, and purpose. We want our lives to matter. Beliefs can be influenced when this deeper motivation is addressed, rather than focusing on less crucial beliefs about life. The destiny question can be framed in different ways for different people. For those outside the kingdom, ask: "What do you think is the purpose of your life?" For disciples, ask: "What is your place and purpose in the kingdom of God? What is your life calling from God?" A best practice of many catalytic leaders is to give answers from the Bible and challenge people to align their lives with them in ways that address the "destiny question."

Best Practice #2: Help others to reflect on the consequences of their beliefs and lifestyles. People need to feel dissatisfaction with their status quo before they become open to embracing new beliefs. Compare the general message: "Developing a healthy diet with lots of vegetables and fruit is important" with a doctor's diagnosis: "You are overweight and developing high blood pressure; unless you change your diet significantly, these could kill you soon."

Asking respectful questions is one of the best ways to help others consider the consequences of their beliefs and lifestyles. For example, in our movement in Sudan, the questions I asked Muslim leaders included: "Is the way you live bringing you the peace you hope for?" "You tell me how badly your Arab brothers in Islam have been treating you. Are you sure you want to continue to be part of such a family?" "You have conflict all around. Can you see that you need peace with God in your heart?"

(Best Practices #1 and #2 share a common approach: non-confrontational communication. It is not belief against belief, mine against yours, with mine being more convincing or superior. Instead, the focus is on addressing and challenging root beliefs. This is done indirectly by telling stories and by asking questions that enable self-discovery. Once a root belief is influenced, other beliefs will realign automatically.)

Best Practice #3: Communicate core beliefs and values concisely, consistently, and constantly. Of all the 106 questions we asked catalytic leaders in our surveys, the item that showed the strongest positive correlation with movement catalyzing was the statement: *I regularly communicate my most important values and beliefs to others.* No other behavior of catalytic leaders correlates more strongly with movement breakthrough. It appears this competency functions as a keystone among all competencies of effective catalytic leaders, and that its proficient practice stands at the very heart of movement ministry. Catalytic leaders exhibit this competency in the following compelling ways, both when reaching those outside the kingdom and when working with teams and partners. They are:

- **Concise:** Catalytic leaders put their core beliefs and values into short memorable phrases. Examples of concise formulation of big and bold visions from catalysts include: "100 million Muslims," "the whole nation for Christ," "reach everyone," "no place left" (without a church), or "fourth generation churches by year X." Some short memorable phrases that people around me hear me say frequently include: "Love God, love the person in front of you"; "Do less but better"; "Go slow to go fast"; "Every problem contains an opportunity"; "In every situation there's something to learn"; "We teach what we know but reproduce who we are"; "Simpler, so it's reproducible"; and "What one thing is most important right now?" Short phrases I share with Muslims constantly include: "Do you want peace with God? The Qur'an says Jesus is the prophet of peace"; and "Do you want guidance and light? The Qur'an says you find it in the Injil." Short phrases I share with secular people constantly include: "Where are you on your spiritual journey?"; and "Try talking to God. He may answer you." In addition to concise statements, catalytic leaders have more elaborate explanations of core beliefs ready to share at any time, often using a mental image and a story.

- **Consistent:** Catalytic leaders use the same phrases, with the same people, repeatedly. Often people need to hear such phrases seven times before they begin internalizing them. When used consistently, they become edifying "mantras."

- **Constant:** Catalytic leaders share their core beliefs at every opportune or inopportune moment. The rule of thumb is: If you are not tired of sharing your beliefs, you likely don't communicate them often enough. One catalyst reports, "We repeat our key statements until people say them in their dreams!"

From Experience: A Practical Method to Influence Other's Beliefs—PAPAI

I have practiced *influencing others' beliefs* about ten thousand times. As I evaluated, experimented, adapted, and thus honed my skill over the years, I developed the PAPAI approach. (To help you remember PAPAI, it's Portuguese for *papa* or *dad*.)

The five letters of PAPAI stand for these five steps:
- Passion for a subject
- Affection for the person(s)
- Presence
- Attachment love
- Initiating dialog.

Let's look at the five steps one by one.

Passion for a subject: The only way to influence others is through passion for what we want to influence them with. Aristotle said that effective communication needs not only *logos* (the words or message) but also *pathos* (passion). So, before we start talking, we need to cultivate passion for the theme in our hearts.

Affection for the person(s): Our effort to influence is misguided and will fall flat unless we feel affection in our hearts for the person(s) we desire to influence. Affection is not simply theoretical love

("Of course I have their best interest at heart"); it carries feelings of valuing and appreciating the person.

Presence: We need to be fully present in the moment and give others our undivided attention. We turn our bodies toward others, focus our minds on them, and engage our soul with them. Undivided attention has been called the "most valuable commodity of the 21st century,"[3] and we must acknowledge that this holds true in Christian ministry.

Attachment love: Developing attachment love means being motivated by love to establish rapport, build a bond, and create "togetherness," so that those we intend to influence sense an attachment with us. Humans are naturally hardwired to quickly fall into a "me versus you" and "us versus them" posture. Holding such a posture naturally triggers an antagonistic response: fight or flight. Jim Wilder describes this as "enemy mode," in which most people live much of the time.[4] Only when we first overcome this posture and create a safe space through attachment love, can we begin the next step.

Initiating dialog: We desire to influence, so we initiate a dialog, with the intention to influence others' beliefs. We do this in a bi-directional communication mode (giving and receiving) rather than one-directional ("preachy") mode. While desiring to influence, we are open to being influenced ourselves by others. This way the PAPAI process has a transformational impact on others and may turn out to be transformational for us as well, as we process what we're hearing through the lens of Scripture.

A GROWTH PATH TO INFLUENCING OTHERS' BELIEFS

To grow in *influencing others' beliefs*, you can take these specific steps, gleaned from the lives of catalytic leaders:

- Formulate in your own words how you can address the "destiny question" with people outside the kingdom and with disciples, in a way they can relate to.
- Actively seek out opportunities to discuss the consequences of people's beliefs and lifestyles.
- Internalize and practice the PAPAI method.

- Identify your own core beliefs and values. Summarize each in a single concise and compelling sentence or phrase.
- Constantly communicate these belief and value statements.
- When you communicate these statements to others, watch their responses. When any statement creates resonance in their hearts, you will normally see it reflected on their faces.
- Keep using the statements that create a response.
- Drop the statements that do not create a response; formulate a different statement for that particular belief or value.
- Go through this process for your personal core beliefs and values, then go through the same process with your core team.
- When you are tired of communicating, keep doing it anyway.

Maximizing Your Chapter Takeaways

Recap

- The ability to influence others' beliefs is a key factor that correlates with movement breakthrough.
- In the book of Acts, beliefs and convictions were influenced by Paul's actions.
- The best practices of catalytic leaders to influence others' beliefs are addressing the destiny question, considering the consequences of beliefs and lifestyles with people, and communicating core beliefs and values concisely, consistently, and constantly.
- Using the PAPAI method—which includes passion for a subject, affection for the person(s), presence, attachment love, and initiating dialog—can be transformational.

Reconnect

Pause for a minute, connect again in your heart with the Father, and pray: *Father, please show me how you want me to live out what I've learned in this chapter, so I can align with your ways and partner with you more fully. Amen.*

Record

- The key insights God has given me in this chapter are:

Reflect More Deeply

Use the following self-coaching questions for prayerful personal or team reflection:

- Before reading this chapter, what was my perception of what I could contribute to influence others' beliefs?
- How can the destiny question best be formulated for people outside the kingdom in our context? How can it best be formulated for fellow disciples?
- What are good topics of conversation in which considering the consequences of people's beliefs and lifestyles together with them could be particularly powerful?
- What are my own core beliefs and values? How could I summarize each of them in one concise and compelling sentence or phrase?
- What elements of the PAPAI method do I already practice consistently? What elements of the PAPAI method have I not been practicing consistently? How can I remind myself to include them in relevant conversations?

Realize

- I sense God nudging me to implement these key insights through the following action steps:
    - Action Step 1

    - Action Step 2

    - Action Step 3

6

Correlating Movement Booster #3

LEADER QUALITY: ASSERTIVENESS

The only healthy communication style is assertive communication.
Jim Rohn

As you prayerfully engage with this chapter, you'll gain a deeper understanding of the following topics:

- *Assertiveness as a key factor:* Discover what it means to be assertive and why it correlates with movement breakthrough.
- *Expressing assertiveness:* Learn practical and healthy ways catalytic leaders are assertive.
- *Growing in being assertive:* Learn and identify steps you can take to grow in this ability.

Before you begin reading this chapter, I encourage you to put the book down, pause, and pray. Connect in your heart with the Father, releasing to him anything that may keep you from being fully present.

Father, please show me what in this chapter you want me to learn and how you want me to grow, so I can align with your ways and partner with you more fully. Amen.

WOW! SO ASSERTIVE!?

A movement catalyst in Southeast Asia shared the following story with me, which describes a heated encounter he had with a new Christ-follower from a Muslim background. Note how the catalyst asserts himself:

> I struggled relentlessly for hours on end with a Sufi sheikh who had become a Christian. I challenged him to return to his people as one of their own to bring them the good news. I countered every argument for hours on end. I prophesied too, that if he makes the sacrifice of living among them again and reaching out to them for the sake of the gospel, just as Paul became like a Jew to the Jews, some of the most important people in the nation will also follow Jesus, and then we will see a massive turning to Christ in his nation. He has nearly committed to do so.... It will probably take several months though ...

Can you feel how strongly the catalyst asserts his conviction toward the sheikh-become-disciple? Listen again to the words he uses to describe this conversation: *struggled, challenged, countered every argument, prophesied* (predicting consequences). How? *Relentlessly.* How long? *Hours on end* in this one encounter. *Several months* more to come.

Without all the details of this situation, it's difficult to assess the appropriateness of such assertiveness. However, the catalytic leader sensed that such assertiveness was needed in this interaction, which had the potential to lead to a nationwide turning to Christ. Assertiveness is required in many encounters to catalyze a movement. Assertiveness characterizes catalytic leaders.

WHAT IS ASSERTIVENESS?

Collins Online Dictionary defines assertive as: "positive or confident in a persistent way."[1] Applied to movement ministry, we used this fuller definition in our research: *Assertiveness is the motivation to influence people and situations, even to the extent of dominating; sharing one's beliefs and convictions clearly so that people take notice and being bold and courageous even when facing opposition and threat.*

- Note, the *motivation* is to influence people and situations toward worthy outcomes. It is not self-assertion for the sake of oneself (self-aggrandizement) nor for the sake of itself (winning for winning's sake). Even though "dominating" can have negative connotations in the contexts of abusive leadership, movement catalysts occasionally are assertive to that extent when the situation demands it.
- The outcome makes it clear whether or not appropriate assertiveness has taken place. People *take notice* and respond, in contrast to much other communication that is merely noise.
- *Opposition and threat* do not stop an assertive leader from being assertive.
- The key activity is *sharing one's beliefs and convictions clearly*. Everyone has great clarity about exactly what the assertive catalytic leader is convinced of and wants to see happen.

MIXED VOICES ON ASSERTIVENESS

Our individual experiences with assertive people influence how we view this trait. However, given it is a characteristic of movement catalysts, it bears further examination. Our perception of assertiveness typically aligns with one of the following three "voices."

Voice #1: Too much assertiveness is bad. Probably all of us have been hurt at some point by an assertive person who came into a situation and steamrolled over everything and everyone. We were left feeling flattened. Hence, most of us have some reservations about assertiveness. Too much of it seems bad. Author Daniel Sinclair echoes this sentiment when describing traits of apostolic leaders: "Areas of the flesh can include self-confidence, over-assertiveness, and independence."[2] Note that Sinclair refers to it as an "area of the flesh," though he is referring to "over-assertiveness," not assertiveness per se. The question is, When does assertiveness become over-assertiveness?

Voice 2: In some cultural contexts, assertiveness is bad. Those of us who are interculturally aware may wonder if assertiveness may be countercultural in some societies, especially in Asian cultures. In fact, in a previous study on catalysts serving among Muslim peoples, I reported: "The trait of assertiveness may depend on the context. It was established that pioneer leaders ministering in Asian societies exhibit a relatively low correlation with assertiveness, because Asian cultures are by nature very indirect and non-assertive. However, pioneer leaders ministering in African societies indeed correlate strongly with assertiveness."[3]

Yet, this observation raised further questions. Consulting with friends who are Asian or minister in Asia gave me valuable insights that challenged my initial conclusions. Assertiveness is expressed in all cultures, including Asian ones. A check of the GLOBE Study, the largest study on cultural values, confirms this.[4] It reports that on a Likert scale of 1–5, most inhabitants of Europe rate lower in assertiveness (between 3.43 and 3.98) than those from Southern Asia (4.17) and Confucian Asia (4.35). Latin Europe (4.31) and Anglo (US and UK, 4.36) do not rate higher than Confucian Asia (4.35).[5]

The research underlying this book verified assertiveness among catalytic leaders who come from and serve in all six mega-cultures of the world, including Asia.

To summarize, assertiveness varies culturally, and in ministry it must be expressed in culturally appropriate ways. We need to find suitable ways to be "positive or confident in a persistent way," as per the general definition of the trait.

Voice 3: There is no leadership without assertiveness. Years ago, when studying for a doctorate in intercultural leadership, I found that all major publications on leadership traits list assertiveness as an essential trait of an effective leader. No leader is effective without assertiveness.

Digging Deeper Into the Research

Ralph Stogdill, an influential author on leadership traits, conducted a qualitative review of 163 trait studies.[6] This review identified characteristics meeting any of these three qualifications: they "differentiate (1) leaders from followers, (2) effective leaders from ineffective leaders, and (3) higher echelon from lower echelon leaders."[7] One of the characteristics, supported by ten or more studies, was assertiveness. Robert House and Mary Baetz analyzed all the empirical studies on leadership traits from the first half of the twentieth century.[8] They identified six leadership traits, among which was prosocial assertiveness (also called dominance). Robert Hogan and colleagues conducted a general review of leadership theory, in which they specifically examined the correlation of personality and leadership effectiveness.[9] They too listed assertiveness as a leadership trait.

Of Christian apostolic leaders, Daniel Sinclair states in no uncertain terms: "They tend not to back down very easily—on anything!"[10] Equally, there is no catalytic leader without the trait of assertiveness. Assertiveness has the highest rating (4.77 on a 1–5 scale, see Table III.1 on page 36) of all traits and competencies that characterize catalytic leaders.

HOW TO INTEGRATE THE DIVERSE VOICES ON ASSERTIVENESS

How can we bring together the diverse voices on assertiveness? "Assertiveness, yes, but not too much of it." "Assertiveness, yes, but in appropriate cultural expressions." "Assertiveness, yes; and not too little."

Leadership researchers Daniel Ames and Francis Flynn help us articulate this somewhat complex dynamic. They describe the relationship between assertiveness and effectiveness as "curvilinear."[11]

Figure 6.1 clarifies their meaning.[12] A leader who exhibits low assertiveness (x-axis) will also have low leadership effectiveness (y-axis). With increasing assertiveness exhibited, leadership effectiveness also increases but only up to a certain point. If assertiveness continues to rise (beyond 3 in the chart), leadership effectiveness begins to decline. A leader can show too little assertiveness or too much; both leave them with limited leadership effectiveness. The golden range of "just the right amount" of assertiveness yields the greatest leadership impact.

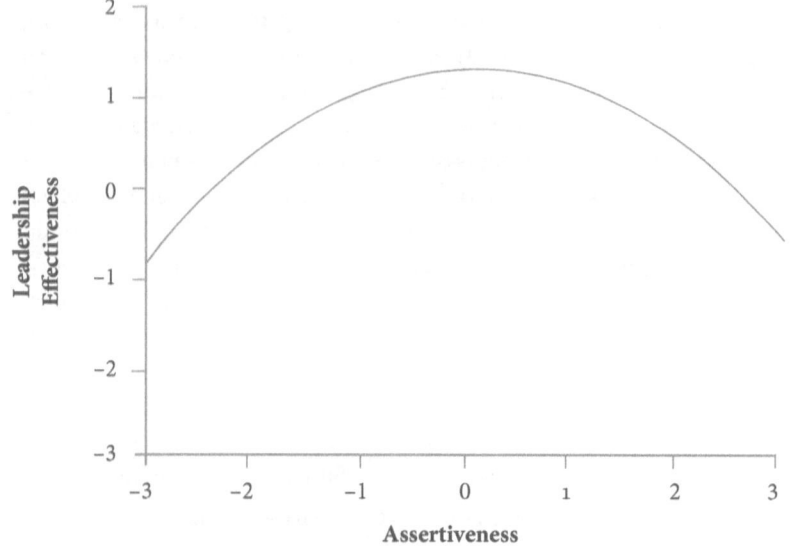

Figure 6.1: Assertiveness and Leadership Effectiveness[13]

What determines the "golden range"? Figure 6.2 depicts the relevant realities that need consideration.[14] The first relevant reality is "change outcomes." This is the measure of change we want to bring about, which is why we express assertiveness. The second reality that must be considered equally is "relational outcomes." When expressing a certain measure of assertiveness, how will that affect the relationship? Figure 6.2 shows three ranges.

Range 1: Too little assertiveness yields too little change, plus the relational outcomes are not good because others will likely lose respect for the catalytic leader and will not perceive them as someone by whom they are inclined to be influenced.

Range 2: More assertiveness yields more change, plus the relational outcomes increase, as others respect the catalytic leader more and will be inclined toward receptivity to their influence.

Range 3: If assertiveness continues to increase, we reach the realm of too much assertiveness, which leads to the change outcomes being maximized, but at a huge price—negative relational outcomes and damaged and weakened relationships—meaning the overall outcome is no longer positive.

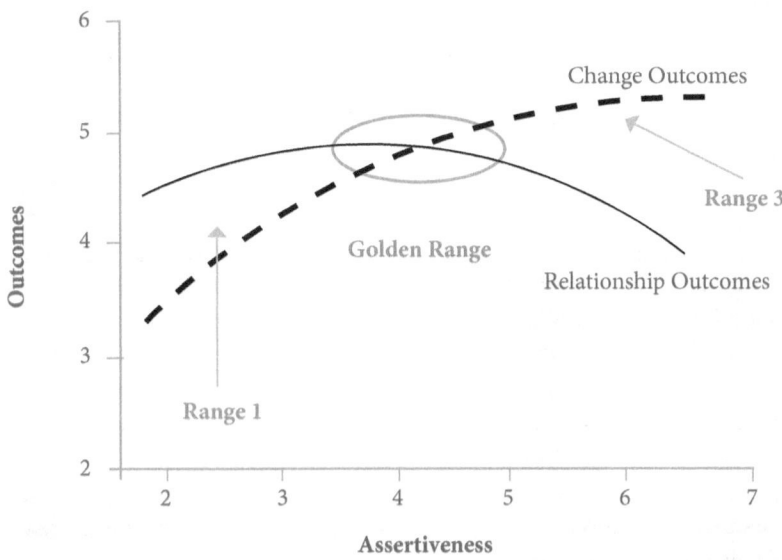

Figure 6.2: The Golden Range of Assertiveness[15]

In summary: the more assertiveness, the more change outcomes will be achieved. However, positive relational outcomes require a healthy middle ground between too little and too much assertiveness.

IDENTIFYING THE "GOLDEN RANGE" OF ASSERTIVENESS

Where the golden range sits depends on the recipients, their previous experience with assertiveness, and their social expectations. For example, for those in lower-power distance cultures, most Asians, someone raised by a despotic father, or someone who has been hurt by a domineering leader, the golden range will generally be on the lower end of the spectrum. For anyone from a society with high-power distance, most Africans, or anyone from a culture with direct communication, the golden range tends to be more toward the higher end of the spectrum of assertiveness.

Practically, where the golden range lies in your sphere of influence will be determined by the sweet spot of those to whom you relate. As a catalytic leader, it's essential to understand your golden range for assertiveness.

From Experience: Learning the Hard Way

I learned to become more assertive the hard way, through trial and error. Sadly, I made my share of mistakes, being too assertive at times and, in the process, hurting people (to whom I have apologized). At other times, I didn't have the courage to be as assertive as the situation demanded, and so I missed opportunities. Yet, apparently, I have grown enough that the Father would use me to start a movement. Over many years, I learned how to apply assertiveness in healthy measures. Authors Ames and Flynn helped me articulate the intuitive sense I had developed. As they describe, unassertive people often fear that if they push any harder, they will incur relational costs, and I found myself with that fear. They also report that, on the other hand, highly assertive leaders don't judge their own behavior as especially assertive and thus don't see it as potentially hurtful or damaging for relationships. Such leaders are primarily concerned about potential loss of change impact. I also found myself in that category occasionally. This increased self-awareness greatly helped me to exert assertiveness more wisely.

At the end of the day, fears about too much or too little assertiveness are irrelevant. Effective leadership is always situational and contingent on followers' preferences. Therefore, the behavior we as catalytic leaders choose must be contingent on the unique situation and the people involved. As catalysts, we must avoid the temptation to relinquish assertiveness for the gospel in order to fit in. We must also abandon assertiveness when it is used primarily to get "our way."

GUIDELINES FOR APPLYING ASSERTIVENESS IN EFFECTIVE AND HEALTHY DOSAGES

- **Pick your battles:** Know when it really matters to influence someone, and when it is okay to be accommodating. In the story at the beginning of this chapter, the catalytic leader felt the stakes were such that the future of the nation hinged on him convincing the Muslim-sheikh-turned-disciple.
- **Determine the appropriate measure of assertiveness:** Ask yourself, *How assertive must I be to achieve the change outcomes to get us closer to movement?* and *How assertive can I be to ensure good relational outcomes?*
- **"Ride" and "relax":** A healthy and productive approach involves a rhythmic balance between asserting yourself ("ride"), followed by inviting others to respond ("relax"). By maintaining this rhythm, you can maintain rapport and achieve your goals.
- **Never endanger the relationship:** Being overly assertive may bring a "win" and provide a short-term gain, yet it may harm a relationship, resulting in a long-term loss.

GROWTH PATH TO ASSERTIVENESS

Here are specific steps you can take to grow in *assertiveness*, gleaned from the lives of catalytic leaders:

- Dare and choose to be assertive.
- Try in certain situations to be a little more assertive than you have been in the past. Then evaluate the outcomes on change and relationships. Experiment to find your golden range. Take a small step toward greater assertiveness.
- Identify the *situations* that truly matter—the watershed moments—by asking yourself, *How high are the stakes of this situation for our long-term vision?* Be assertive in those situations. The higher the stakes, the more assertiveness is likely required.

- Identify the *issues* that truly matter—the game changers—and be assertive in them. In order to identify these issues, ask yourself: *What issue would take us closer to movement if I addressed it? What issue could block a movement if I didn't address it?*
- Invite feedback from trusted sources on your assertiveness. Ask: "In your assessment, how effective was my approach to bringing about the needed change? How do you feel relationships were affected?"

Maximizing Your Chapter Takeaways

Recap

- Assertiveness is a key correlating factor that leads to movement breakthrough.
- Catalytic leaders express assertiveness in healthy ways— strong enough to lead to desired change outcomes, yet not so strong as to damage relationships.
- The golden range of assertiveness is determined by the recipients and their previous experience with assertiveness plus their social expectations.

Reconnect

Pause for a minute, connect again in your heart with the Father, and pray: *Father, please show me how you want me to live out what I've learned in this chapter, so I can align with your ways and partner with you more fully. Amen.*

Record

- The key insights God has given me in this chapter are:

Reflect More Deeply

Use the following self-coaching questions for prayerful personal or team reflection:

- How assertive (or not) am I naturally? Do I tend to err on the side of being over-assertive, sometimes in danger of steam-rolling people? Or do I tend to err on the side of not being assertive enough, in danger of missing opportunities to speak up and exert influence?
- What was a situation in the recent past that truly mattered for our ministry, in which I needed to be very assertive? Was I? If not, what kept me from being more assertive in the moment? What can I learn for a future similar situation?
- What could it look like to experiment with being a bit more assertive than I have been? What might be a good situation for practice in the coming weeks?
- What is an issue that could take us closer to movement if I addressed it? What would it look like to assertively exert influence in that matter?

Realize

- I sense God nudging me to implement these key insights through the following action steps:
    - Action Step 1

    - Action Step 2

    - Action Step 3

7

Correlating Movement Booster #4

EFFECTIVE MINISTRY STRATEGY

*The missionary strategy of the Apostles was guided,
directed and controlled by the Holy Spirit.*

William F. Kumuyi

As you prayerfully engage with this chapter, you'll gain a deeper understanding of the following topics:

- *Strategy as a key factor:* Discover why developing an effective ministry strategy is essential for movements.
- *The six elements of strategy development:* Learn how to develop an effective strategy for your ministry by considering the six essential elements.

Before you begin reading this chapter, I encourage you to put the book down, pause, and pray. Connect in your heart with the Father, releasing to him anything that may keep you from being fully present.

Father, please show me what in this chapter you want me to learn and how you want me to grow, so I can align with your ways and partner with you more fully. Amen.

THE SIGNIFICANCE OF DEVELOPING AN EFFECTIVE MINISTRY STRATEGY

In addition to leader *qualities*, we wanted to assess other *factors* boosting movement success. One of those *factors* is effective ministry strategy.

My team and I asked pioneers to rate "to what extent developing the right ministry strategy or method contributed to the catalyzing of their movement." The average rating of the catalytic leaders was remarkably high: 4.51 on a Likert scale of 1–5, compared to 3.71 for the pioneer church planters who had not catalyzed a movement. Both catalysts and non-catalysts commented in the interviews that frustration with existing traditional ministry methods led them to experiment with new forms of outreach. Courage is required to break free from the shackles of church tradition or to challenge traditional ministry methods, especially in the face of opposition from other Christians. This quote from the catalyst of a huge ongoing movement in South Asia describes the early days of his ministry:

> I said, "What is it we're doing wrong? Why are they rejecting the gospel?" I looked at the culture and looked at the language and our dependency on Western money. It was so power-controlled, and the funders were telling people what to do. I said, "How about doing it the other way round, and letting the people discover what to do by the help of the Holy Spirit?" I was also thinking about the gender issue. At that time only men could baptize people.... Did Jesus give the Great Commission only to men or to all? Is obedience only for men or for all? In those days I had more questions than answers. If I asked anyone, people in the ministry were very defensive, and no one was willing to give me an answer.

In this catalyst's case, willingness to try new approaches eventually led to a tremendous harvest of new disciples that continues to multiply to this day. Other catalytic leaders also discovered that what others thought were ineffective ministry approaches proved to be right for their particular context. The catalyst of a substantial movement in

Southeast Asia commented, "What everybody else says, 'Don't do'—that usually works in our case!"

THE KEY ELEMENTS OF AN EFFECTIVE STRATEGY

Most often an effective strategy in movements follows two essential principles. First, it is God-inspired. An effective strategy takes into account and is built on the vision God has already given. Second, an effective strategy is never a "copy and paste" from another context. It is tailored for the unique ministry context, addressing the felt needs of the community being reached.

Therefore, for the development of your own God-inspired and tailored strategy for your ministry, six key elements need consideration and clarification:

1. **Vision:** What has God spoken?
2. **Target audience:** Who are we reaching?
3. **Addressing needs:** How can we address their felt needs?
4. **Seeking God's guidance:** How do we find those who are spiritually open?
5. **Reproducibility:** How do we make everything reproducible?
6. **Evaluation and adaptation:** How do we evaluate and adapt regularly?

A PATHWAY FOR DEVELOPING EACH KEY ELEMENT

Catalytic leaders take into consideration all six elements in developing an effective strategy for their context. The following steps have proven to be helpful in processing these elements with a team.

Vision—Discern What God has Said

- Record all revelations (Scriptures, prophetic words, dreams, or visions) we have received from God about our calling (how God intends to partner with us).

- Record revelations we have received from God about what he intends to do among the people we're reaching.
- Reflect on how these revelations can bolster our expectant faith and what we are believing God for in prayer.
- Seek clarity about how these revelations inform what ministries we engage in and how we do ministry.

Target Audience—Know Who We Are Reaching

- Identify the community we feel called to reach, describing them as specifically as possible.
- Understand their particular beliefs and religious practices.
- Identify their felt needs materially (more applicable in developing countries), psychologically (more applicable in developed countries), socially, and spiritually. Identify the life issues they struggle with: their pain points, dissatisfactions, unanswered questions, and brokenness.
- Identify the power holders and influencers that need to be won so the community can come into the kingdom.
- Learn about the social networks through which the gospel can travel.

Address Needs—Express Tangible Love

- Strategize how to meet people's felt needs holistically in everyday life, in order to express tangible love to them.
- Choose what kind of compassion ministry would meet their felt needs and be most conducive to a movement.
- Identify which of people's beliefs are true, so we can use them as common ground to communicate the good news in receptor-oriented ways, building on their beliefs.
- Formulate the gospel for them in light of their felt spiritual needs, so they perceive it as good news for them.

Seek God's Guidance—Find Those Who Are Spiritually Open

- Develop a radiant spirituality that is visible in the community and attractive to people.
- Determine how will we live so we are respected, likeable, and expressing tangible love and care to people.
- Find out the topics that people talk about all the time in everyday conversations, and craft statements that turn these everyday conversations into gospel conversations.
- Plan how to use (social) media to extend our reach beyond our social networks, in order to find those who are open to religious change.

Reproducibility—Make Everything Replicable

- Make everything reproducible from day one, considering the *messenger*, *message*, *methods* and *materials*.
  - **Messenger:** Develop a lifestyle that can be emulated by seekers and disciples.
  - **Message:** Communicate the good news in forms that can easily be passed on: Accommodate oral learner preferences and use Bible storying, a discovery approach, local folk tales, and proverbs.
  - **Methods:** Develop replicable methods that enable local leaders to reproduce the strategies independently in a new location.
    - Identify the core spiritual DNA to be instilled in our disciples.
    - Create simple, recurring, and replicable formats for groups.
    - Equip and empower local disciples to lead effectively.
    - Make all initiatives and activities financially self-sustainable.
  - **Materials:** Make all materials reproducible, by keeping them simple, so our disciples can use them with the next generation of disciples.

- Adjust materials for oral-preference learners.
- Ensure the materials anchor our disciples in the Bible.
- In most movements, make discipleship materials that have the following simple format:
  i. A relevant Scripture passage for each topic
  ii. A few simple observation and application questions

Evaluation and Adaption—Review, Reflect, and Innovate

- Plan how frequently we will pause—to seek God to give us more revelation, and to reflect deeply in order to gain insights that will inform our strategy.
- Identify the key evaluation points that will show us if we are making progress toward a movement.
- Ensure we remain radical learners, continue to try new things, and innovate.

From Experience: An Example of Developing an Effective Strategy

Foundational to developing our ministry strategy was the dream God had given me that he would write church history and there would be a movement one day. In developing our strategy we kept asking the question, "What will it take to see that dream realized?" In broad strokes, we determined that in order to start a movement, we would need to reach the power holders in society—the village chiefs, imams, and rebel army commanders. We identified ourselves as people of God from the very first encounter, making it publicly known that we were spiritual people. We addressed the felt needs of the war-affected communities through mobile clinics and a feeding program. We lived a radiant spirituality, both through expressing love in tangible ways and by praying in public and turning (almost) every conversation into a Jesus conversation. The latter helped us to quickly identify those who were spiritually open. We took the approach of steering those leaders who were open toward a group conversion, rather than targeting individuals, which could yield quick "wins" but likely cause friction that would hinder a movement. We tried to make everything as reproducible as possible, using a discovery-storying approach and giving the oral learners Scriptures on audio files. And we kept evaluating and adapting in the entire process.

Maximizing Your Chapter Takeaways

Recap

- To see movement breakthrough, an effective strategy must be built on what God has spoken—on the vision he has revealed.
- Catalytic leaders adapt their strategy for the unique ministry context, addressing the felt needs of the community.
- Catalytic leaders consider six elements for strategy development.

Reconnect

Pause for a minute, connect again in your heart with the Father, and pray: *Father, please show me how you want me to live out what I've learned in this chapter, so I can align with your ways and partner with you more fully. Amen.*

Record

- The key insights God has given me in this chapter are:

- The questions I have for deeper reflection are:

Realize

- I sense God nudging me to implement these key insights through the following action steps:
    - Action Step 1

    - Action Step 2

    - Action Step 3

8

Correlating Movement Booster #5

DISCOVERY-GROUP APPROACH

God created truth; we discover it.

The John Ankerberg Show

As you prayerfully engage with this chapter, you'll gain a deeper understanding of the following topics:

- *The discovery approach as a key factor:* Understand the powerful principles behind the discovery approach that make it so transformational in movement breakthrough.
- *Implementing the discovery approach:* Learn how to use discovery more consistently in catalyzing movements.
- *Jesus' use of discovery:* Explore how Jesus guided people toward self-discovery.

Before you begin reading this chapter, I encourage you to put the book down, pause, and pray. Connect in your heart with the Father, releasing to him anything that may keep you from being fully present.

Father, please show me what in this chapter you want me to learn and how you want me to grow, so I can align with your ways and partner with you more fully. Amen.

THE SIGNIFICANCE OF THE DISCOVERY-GROUP APPROACH FOR MOVEMENTS

We asked the pioneers in our study to what extent using a "discovery approach and discovery groups" contributed to the catalyzing of their movement or their ministry fruitfulness. The effective catalysts' average rating (on a scale of 1–5) was 4.16, once again significantly higher than the non-catalysts' rating (3.45).

The discovery approach leverages the principle that self-discovered truth is more deeply owned and internalized than truth that is taught and passively received. This concept is supported by contemporary learning theories.[1]

Jesus himself used the discovery approach more than we who have grown up used to Sunday morning sermons realize. The Gospels record Jesus asking 307 questions toward self-discovery. By comparison, each of the four Synoptic Gospels record only five sermons. The Gospels also record Jesus being asked 183 questions. Of these, Jesus answers only three![2] Apparently, instead of giving people all the answers, Jesus preferred to guide people toward self-discovery.

Movement catalysts frequently share stories of the importance of the discovery approach, as our research confirms. One West African catalyst shared how a miraculous healing paved the way for a Discovery Bible Study (DBS), which in turn led to multiplication of the church. A woman, whose father was an imam, had been paralyzed for several years. A mission team reaching out in her village connected with her. "Over time she experienced a dramatic miracle: She could stand up! This opened doors to the family and community. We started DBS, engaging people with God's Word. This lady now leads two or three groups herself."

A catalytic leader in Southeast Asia explained that his movement's only strategy is Discovery Bible Studies. "We don't preach sermons; we just tell Bible stories and have questions and discussions. You don't have to have a formula to do that." A rapidly growing movement has ensued from these discovery groups.

THE POWERFUL PRINCIPLES BEHIND THE DISCOVERY APPROACH

In many movements, group meetings have the following standard elements:

- **Fellowship:** sharing of joys and struggles
- **Worship:** thanking God specifically for what group members are grateful for
- **Prayer:** for specific needs of the group and non-disciples that group members reach out to
- **Bible study**: using a discovery approach, culminating in
  - o *Obedience:* commitment to take a specific step in the coming week
  - o *Evangelism*: commitment to share with someone in the coming week
- **Accountability:** asking and sharing with one another about the obedience and evangelism steps

Although discovery groups share several common elements with small groups in traditional churches, they uniquely emphasize obedience, evangelism, and accountability—crucial aspects that are usually absent in most small groups in legacy churches. These three elements lie at the very heart of discipleship; without them, healthy formation of disciples is seriously impaired.

Examining how different ways of "doing church" impact learning reveals the transformative power of discovery groups. Educators refer to a concept called the "implicit curriculum"—the things that are taught implicitly through the way teaching and learning happen.[3] Educators commonly agree that the implicit curriculum has a more profound effect than what is taught in the explicit curriculum.[4] The concept of the implicit curriculum offers a valuable framework for comparing the discovery-group approach with a traditional Sunday morning service or small group. To understand the impact of these models, we must consider how they shape learning by what values they implicitly convey—see table 8.1 for a comparison.

Table 8.1: Comparison of Traditional vs. Discovery-Group Approach

Element	Traditional Approach	Discovery Approach
Bible	Only truly understood by a few; better served as a ready-made meal	Accessible; every disciple can understand though the Spirit's inspiration; intended to nourish the heart of any disciple who reads and meditates on it
Holy Spirit	Speaks mainly through a few professionals or clergy	Speaks to all disciples through the Bible and through other disciples
God's speaking to and communing with his people	Through a mediator	Directly
Priesthood of all believers	Limited to corporate worship and prayer	A reality lived every time believers gather together—both in relating to God and fellow-believers
Leaders	Professionals who feed the flock and perform the ministry themselves	Ordinary disciples equipped for ministry
Spiritual fellowship	Sharing discoveries of truth, commitments to obey, and accountability as optional add-ons after the actual service	Sharing discoveries of truth, commitments to obey, and accountability as the heart of the gathering
Discipleship	Listening to the truth someone else discovered, resulting in merely optional obedience	Obedience to the truth one discovers

This leads us to explore what the discovery model offers, in contrast with what the traditional model lacks. We often mistakenly assume that when something is missing, it is simply absent, leaving a void. However, the absence of certain elements reveals as much as the presence of others. In learning theory, this is known as the "null curriculum."[5] The absence of concrete obedience, regular gospel sharing, and accountability in traditional small-group approaches communicates that such practices aren't important. Their absence conveys: "We value fellowship, worship, prayer, and Bible study. Gaining some new insights through studying the Bible is great, but concrete obedience to biblical teaching is optional. You needn't prioritize immediately sharing with someone outside the kingdom. And we won't hold you accountable because follow-through doesn't really matter. We're happy if you demonstrate your faithfulness by showing up again next week." Although no pastor or small group leader would explicitly state this, the null curriculum unwittingly and nonverbally communicates this. In discovery groups, obedience, evangelism, and accountability are actively practiced, instilling spiritual values and developing essential discipleship habits.

From Experience: Buzzing with Discovery

During the early days of my movement ministry, David Watson hadn't yet popularized Discovery Bible Study. However, I had developed a very similar method, geared to oral learners. In hindsight, I would call it "Discovery Bible Storying." Our approach was to tell a Bible story and then ask several in the group to retell it. We had them repeat it many times, until we felt they retained it with certain accuracy. We then asked simple inductive Bible study questions, so they would communally discover and understand the story's deeper meanings. Toward the end, we would ask, "And how can we follow this story?"

People were captivated by the stories. And, as Muslims who had only memorized the Qur'an and its teaching but never really understood it, the discovery questions prompted them to ponder religious matters for the first time. They enjoyed grasping the meaning of the gospel. One market day we had an extended lunch break, and group members returned to the discipleship meeting with excitement: "The market is buzzing with your stories!" They had immediately shared the new stories with others.

Maximizing Your Chapter Takeaways

Recap

- To see movement breakthrough, catalytic leaders adopt the discovery-group approach, which has a strong transformational function.
- Instead of giving people answers, Jesus often preferred to guide people toward self-discovery.
- The discovery-group model addresses the shortcomings of the traditional church model by emphasizing concrete obedience, immediate gospel sharing, and accountability.

Reconnect

Pause for a minute, connect again in your heart with the Father, and pray: *Father, please show me how you want me to live out what I've learned in this chapter, so I can align with your ways and partner with you more fully. Amen.*

Record

- The key insights God has given me in this chapter are:

Reflect More Deeply

Use the following self-coaching questions for prayerful personal or team reflection:

- How significantly does discovery-based discipleship and training feature in our current ministry approach?
- In what areas can we give discovery a more prominent place in our ministry?
- How can we identify whether some of our leaders are reverting to traditional approaches with an overemphasis on preaching and presenting?
- How well do I personally model the discovery approach in my own teaching and training?

Realize

- I sense God nudging me to implement these key insights through the following action steps:
    - Action Step 1

    - Action Step 2

    - Action Step 3

9

Correlating Movement Booster #6

EFFECTIVELY RAISING UP LEADERS

If you are short on the bench today, that means your predecessors were asleep at the wheel 10 to 15 years ago, tending exclusively to the business of that day. If today you do not build a leadership development system, your successors will not have adequate bench strength to succeed.

Michael Lombardy and Robert Eichinger

As you prayerfully engage with this chapter, you'll gain a deeper understanding of the following topics:

- *The importance of strong, indigenous leaders:* Discover why effectively raising up leaders is essential for movement growth and sustainability.
- *Training and mentoring:* Learn how movements develop their leaders' character and competence.

Before you begin reading this chapter, I encourage you to put the book down, pause, and pray. Connect in your heart with the Father, releasing to him anything that may keep you from being fully present.

Father, please show me what in this chapter you want me to learn and how you want me to grow, so I can align with your ways and partner with you more fully. Amen.

EFFECTIVELY RAISING UP LEADERS AS THE ·PILLARS OF THE MOVEMENT

As noted earlier, leadership expert John Maxwell writes: "Everything rises and falls on leadership."[1] Applied to movements, a movement rises when local leaders are raised up effectively. Similar to ancient Greek and Roman buildings that stood on strong pillars, the more pillars, and the stronger the pillars, the bigger the building can become. The more leaders, and the stronger the leaders, the bigger the movement can become.

Sustained movements are always indigenous. This means that raising up local leaders is vital—the factor catalytic leaders rated most highly in boosting movement breakthrough (4.55). This distinguishes catalysts from non-catalysts, who rated this factor much lower (averaging 3.75) in boosting ministry fruitfulness.

Effective catalytic leaders raise up local leaders from day one. A West African movement has grown tremendously this way, as one expatriate catalyst describes: "It's not us. It's the two nationals we've trained who are doing the work at this point. These two local people have catalyzed a movement that now has over 3,300 groups."

The primary approaches catalytic leaders use to empower local leaders are *training* and *mentoring*.

An analysis of training in many movements reveals that it usually aims to develop both character and competence.[2] Training therefore not only incorporates core biblical concepts but also equips individuals to live as disciples and make new ones. Three key values define this training approach: a solid biblical foundation; the trainers' example; and a commitment to simple, reproducible, and continuous training formats. One trainee in a movement in West Africa put it like this: "Our leaders have never stopped training and teaching us. Training must be continuous."

Training is often coupled with mentoring. Mentoring involves a relationship between a leader and a mentee. Through individual guidance, the mentor helps develop the mentee's character and competence. Mentoring is often initiated by a leader selecting a mentee who demonstrates favorable character—an individual who leads by example. This individual is then guided not only in personal growth but also what it means to be a leader. Mentoring is viewed as a crucial leadership function. It's considered essential for all leaders to engage in this practice, providing guidance and support to their mentees.

A variety of approaches are used for mentoring, including peer-group learning, the discovery approach, and doing ministry together. The mentee is introduced to leadership by gradual delegation of responsibilities, which usually leads to complete delegation in the mentor's absence. Progress reviews play an important role in monitoring progress and discerning areas for improvement, shaping future mentoring topics. Key values of effective mentoring include joint prayer; spending time together; expressing care, love, and affirmation; sensitivity to individual gifting and progress; correction; and role modeling. Mentoring is significant for the transference of spiritual DNA, which is essential for healthy movement growth.

From Experience: Raising Leaders to Address a Bottleneck

At one point in my movement journey, our team realized that our lack of local leaders was a bottleneck to further growth. The number of disciples kept growing; the number of house churches in ever more villages kept growing; but the leaders necessary to shepherd those new house churches kept lagging behind. We needed to address this. We concluded that raising up local leaders needed to become the focus of our efforts. We developed several training modules and invited the emerging leaders from fifty locations to gather regionally for three to four days at a time. The intense time spent together created the opportunity to build deeper trust relationships, which formed the basis for ongoing mentoring. This greatly strengthened the movement. With hindsight, we could also see that this essential change made the movement self-sustainable.

SIX ELEMENTS, ONE LASER-SHARP FOCUS

To sum up, the data is clear:

Three *qualities* of the catalytic leader correlate with movement breakthrough:

- Deep prayer
- Influencing others' beliefs
- Assertiveness

In addition, three *ministry factors* correlate with movement breakthrough:

- Developing an effective strategy
- Using a discovery approach and discovery groups
- Effectively raising up leaders

Although these six elements are not the only ones, they correlate most directly with movement outcomes. To aim for movement breakthrough, you'll need a laser-sharp focus of your efforts on these six elements.

Maximizing Your Chapter Takeaways

Recap

- How effectively we raise up leaders determines how broad the movement can grow.
- The primary approaches catalytic leaders use are training and mentoring in both character and competence.

Reconnect

Pause for a minute, connect again in your heart with the Father, and pray: *Father, please show me how you want me to live out what I've learned in this chapter, so I can align with your ways and partner with you more fully. Amen.*

Record

- The key insights God has given me in this chapter are:

Reflect More Deeply

Use the following self-coaching questions for prayerful personal or team reflection:

- How effective are your current leadership development efforts?
- How can you more fully integrate into your training the approaches and values of *training* in movements?
- How can you more fully integrate into your training the approaches and values of *mentoring* in movements?
- Who are you currently developing, and what equipping do these leaders need to reach their maximum level of fruitfulness?
- Are there any other individuals you want to raise up more intentionally?

Realize

- I sense God nudging me to implement these key insights through the following action steps:
    - Action Step 1

    - Action Step 2

    - Action Step 3

10

ADDITIONAL MOVEMENT BOOSTERS

The best way to handle a situation is not to fake simplicity but to embrace the complexity and clarify it by making it more understandable.

Andrew Hinton

As you prayerfully engage with this chapter, you'll gain a deeper understanding of the following topics:

- *Additional movement boosters:* In addition to the six *correlating* boosters, discover the other ministry factors mentioned most frequently by practitioners as contributing to or boosting movements.
- *The ability of catalysts to influence factors:* Understand how most of the boosting factors are internal—they can be influenced by the catalysts themselves and their teams.

Before you begin reading this chapter, I encourage you to put the book down, pause, and pray. Connect in your heart with the Father, releasing to him anything that may keep you from being fully present.

Father, please show me what in this chapter you want me to learn and how you want me to grow, so I can align with your ways and partner with you more fully. Amen.

FACTORS BOOSTING MOVEMENTS

As noted on page 35, our team wanted to understand the *ministry factors*, other than the *qualities* of the catalyst, that significantly influence the emergence of a movement. Of the twenty-one ministry factors identified, eleven were grouped as "boosting factors." We also categorized these factors as either "internal" or "external." Internal factors are those which can be influenced by the pioneers themselves and their teams, while external factors are those outside their immediate control, which cannot be influenced directly (other than through prayer). Of the eleven boosting ministry factors, we classified eight as internal and three as external.

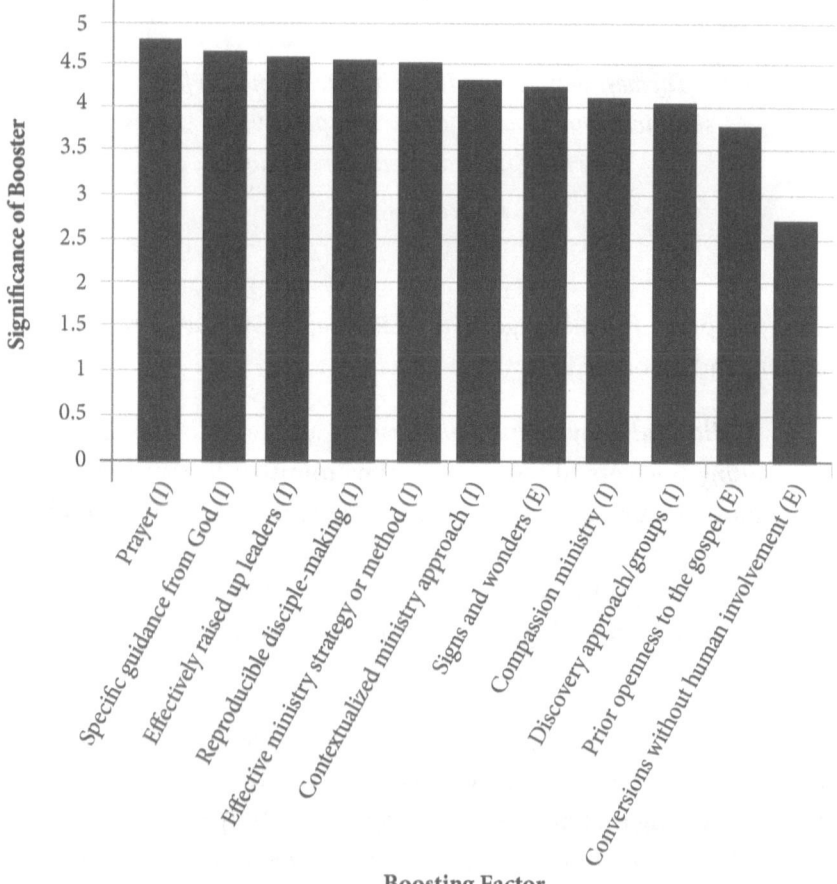

Figure 10.1: Factors Boosting the Catalyzing of
Movements, as Rated by Catalytic Leaders

Survey participants rated the extent to which each factor had impacted their ministry on a Likert scale of 1–5. We asked the effective catalysts: "How much did this factor contribute to/inhibit the catalyzing of your movement?"

Our team examined the eleven factors mentioned most frequently by practitioners as *boosting* movements. Figure 10.1 shows how significant catalytic leaders assessed each factor to be. These are shown in descending order of impact. The "I" in parentheses denotes an internal factor, the "E" an external one.

Prayer ranks at the top of the list. This includes all kinds of prayer—by the catalytic leaders, corporate prayer by their teams and partners, within the emerging movements, and mobilized outside. This gives us empirical evidence that prayer is viewed by catalytic leaders as a primary contributor to the catalyzing of movements. This booster needs to be distinguished from "deep prayer," one of the *leadership qualities* of the catalyst, which we explored in chapter four.

Effective catalysts report specific guidance from God as the second-most-significant factor in their movement catalyzing. This relates to the expectant faith they exhibit, grounded on specific revelation they received from God. Many catalytic leaders report that God spoke to them about his plans for them and their ministry and/or his plans for what he desires to accomplish among the people they serve. A number reported receiving such revelation through a dream, vision, or prophetic word; others through a specific Scripture God gave them. In other words, expectant faith arises from catalytic leaders receiving specific guidance from God.

Noteworthy is that the *external* boosting factors all rank low (signs and wonders) or even very low (prior openness to the gospel and conversions without human involvement). This indicates that factors internal to the catalytic leaders—meaning those over which they have some measure of control—were most significant in catalyzing a movement.

In figure 10.2, each front bar gives the average rating for the non-catalysts, with catalysts' average rating behind them. The figure only shows the seven factors for which the difference between catalysts and non-catalysts was statistically significant. The factors are presented in descending order of difference between catalysts and non-catalysts, from left to right.

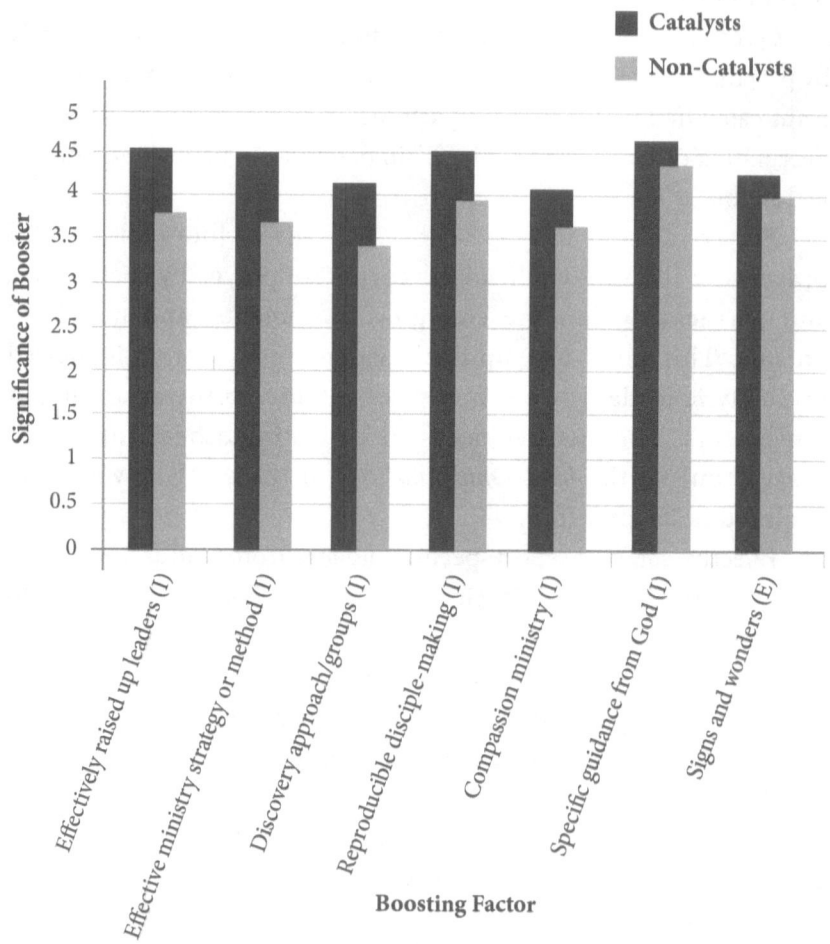

Figure 10.2: Boosting Factors in Comparison

When comparing these seven factors, note that effective catalysts experience every one of the internal factors as contributing more significantly than non-catalysts. Overall, the boosting factors were scored higher by effective catalysts by an average of +0.40. As already noted and explored in chapters six to nine, the difference is most apparent with the following factors: effectively raising up leaders (+0.81), effective ministry strategy or method (+0.80), and the use of discovery approach/groups (+0.72).

All the factors where the ratings of the two groups differ most widely relate to ministry strategy or approach: the three just mentioned, plus reproducible disciple-making (+0.54) and compassion ministry/met holistic needs (+0.50).

Note that six of the seven boosting factors in figure 10.2 are internal. Even the one that is not—signs and wonders—is often significantly impacted by the catalytic leaders, due to exercise of their faith and prayer (or lack thereof).

We can draw two conclusions from the comparisons figure 10.2 illustrates. First, the ratings for the two factors most closely related to the supernatural realm—specific guidance from God and signs and wonders—show the least difference between effective catalysts and non-catalysts (average difference of 0.28). Thus, it would seem that what some call the "God factor" does not offer enough explanation for what sets apart effective catalysts from their peers. Second, the five factors which show the most significant difference (average difference of 0.67) all directly relate to ministry behaviors. God worked supernaturally through the ministries of both effective catalysts and the control group, but what set the former apart had to do with their personal actions.

Interestingly, we found no statistically significant difference between the groups for the boosting factors "prior openness to the gospel" and "conversions without human involvement," even though effective catalysts rated these factors slightly higher than non-catalysts. (For more on the factor of receptivity, see chapter twelve.)

Given the majority of the boosting factors are internal to the pioneers and teams, generating and developing these contributing factors is paramount and distinguishes effective catalysts from non-catalysts.

The overall weight and importance of internal factors in the findings should challenge practitioners to focus on fulfilling their human responsibility and to work on all internal factors under their influence, in a posture of dependence on God's guidance.

FURTHER FACTORS IDENTIFIED IN INTERVIEWS

We wanted to avoid overlooking factors effective catalysts assessed to have impacted their movements. Therefore, in addition to having participants rate the twenty-one ministry factors in the survey, we conducted in-depth interviews, asking them the following: What do you consider the main factors that have significantly *contributed* to the catalyzing of your movement? Please name the three most significant ones.

Answers to this question shed more light on the issue of developing an effective ministry strategy. Catalysts were much more likely to do a number of things than non-catalysts: use a disciple-making movements (DMM) approach, engage in compassion ministry, connect with persons of peace, work through social networks, and use reproducible tools.

The interviews revealed that effective catalysts take a fundamentally different approach to relationship building. Whereas non-catalysts' approach can be categorized as "diffuse relationship building," effective catalysts talked about relationships with the more intentional language of empowerment. They consistently spoke of mentoring, ongoing training, and promoting ministry led by local people.

The interviews also identified the following additional boosting factors, listed in order of the frequency mentioned, from most to least. This list gives us a fuller picture of factors associated with movements, beyond those examined more thoroughly in the survey. Although useful, they carry less significance than the factors listed above in the survey results.

Internal Boosting Factors

- evangelism
- use of local language
- intentional mentoring
- partnering and networking
- team contributions
- example of leaders
- vision casting
- ongoing training
- literature distribution
- persons of peace
- tangible love of ministry team
- financial resources
- oral-ministry approach
- ministry through social networks

External Boosting Factors

- openness to the gospel because of crises
- government freedom for ministry

Maximizing Your Chapter Takeaways

Recap

- In addition to the six correlating movements boosters, practitioners identify other factors as boosting movements.
- Eight of the eleven boosters are internal—they can be influenced by the catalysts themselves and their teams.

Reconnect

Pause for a minute, connect again in your heart with the Father, and pray: *Father, please show me how you want me to live out what I've learned in this chapter, so I can align with your ways and partner with you more fully. Amen.*

Record

- The key insights God has given me in this chapter are:

- The questions I have for deeper reflection are:

Realize

- I sense God nudging me to implement these key insights through the following action steps:
    - Action Step 1

    - Action Step 2

    - Action Step 3

||

THE RIGHT PERSON WITH THE RIGHT METHODS IS WHAT STARTS A MOVEMENT

If someone says to me, give me the method or give me the curriculum, I know that they have not understood that this [the catalyzing of a movement] is accomplished through persons rather than methods.

Bill Smith

As you prayerfully engage with this chapter, you'll gain a deeper understanding of the following topics:

- *The significance of the right person:* Learn about why the right person is needed to start a movement.
- *Movement publications until now:* Explore how previous publications have tended to emphasize movement methodology over the right person.
- *The synergy of person and methods:* Discover the significance of ministry methods used in tandem with the person of the catalyst.

Before you begin reading this chapter, I encourage you to put the book down, pause, and pray. Connect in your heart with the Father, releasing to him anything that may keep you from being fully present.

Father, please show me what in this chapter you want me to learn and how you want me to grow, so I can align with your ways and partner with you more fully. Amen.

WHAT STARTS A MOVEMENT ... OR IS IT *WHO*?

The question of what starts a movement—the right method or the right person—has stirred up more discussion than any of my other publications. Our research from movements has produced the data to show that certain qualities characterize all catalytic leaders. We have also explored the other factors that contribute to and boost movements. These factors are either internal (implemented by the catalytic leaders) or external (having impact that can be mitigated by catalytic leaders). By surveying movements globally, we have revealed that wherever you see a movement, you will find a catalyst with a particular set of qualities. Effective catalysts all over the world have certain traits and competencies in common, which they exhibit consistently.

So, is the right *person* needed to start a movement?

Before we can answer this question, we need to consider that the overwhelming majority of movements (though not all) were catalyzed using certain movement approaches. Is the right *method* needed to start a movement?

Let's allow the data to answer the question. To recap from chapter three, table 11.1 presents the traits and competencies of pioneers effective in catalyzing a movement. The three that show direct correlation with movement breakthrough (see chapters four through six) are italicized.

Table 11.1: The Traits and Competencies of Catalytic Leaders

Personality Traits	Spiritual Traits and Competencies	Social Influence Traits and Competencies
Radical Learning	Hunger for God	Inspiring Personality
Innovation	Listening to God	*Influencing Others' Beliefs*
Drive to Achieve	Evangelistic Zeal	Inspiring Shared Vision
Conscientiousness	Expectant Faith	*Assertiveness*
Personal Agency	*Deep Prayer*	Transformational Disciple-Making
Persistence	Tangible Love	Empowering
Agreeableness	Confidence in Local Disciples	
	Confidence in the Bible	

These twenty-one qualities that enable the catalyzing of a movement characterize all of the 147 catalytic leaders who participated in the study. Among all those studied, we found no catalytic leader who does not consistently exhibit all these catalytic qualities.

So, the data makes it abundantly clear. Wherever you see a movement, you find a catalyst with a particular set of qualities who started it. To start a movement, the right person is needed: a person who exhibits these qualities.

What part then does the right method play?

THE RIGHT MINISTRY METHOD—WHAT OTHERS HAVE SAID

We have established that all catalytic leaders exhibit certain qualities. Before summarizing from previous chapters what the research has found, let us consider the contribution of a few voices in the movement world from whom we all have benefited tremendously. Most literature on the subject of catalyzing a movement has focused on spiritual traits of the catalyst combined with the right methodology. In *Church*

Planting Movements, David Garrison emphasizes characteristics of church-planting movements as well as methodology.[1] At the same time, he ascribes a crucial role to the catalyst: "God has given Christians vital roles to play in the success or failure of these movements."[2]

David and Paul Watson also emphasize right methodology in their book *Contagious Disciple Making*.[3] They describe the significance of the methodological elements of the disciple-making movements approach as follows: "This book focuses on the strategic elements you need to get a movement started. If you remove any of these elements, you won't have a movement, period. You may have some growth, but you won't experience a movement."[4] David Watson, however, also regards the role of the catalyst as critical, since he or she is the one who sparks the process of a movement.[5] Most of Watson's competencies are either verified directly in my research or appear under competencies identified by this research.[6]

The late Steve Smith and Ying Kai likewise emphasized methodology; they presented us with Training for Trainers (T4T), an exhaustive, branded church-planting package. Smith and Kai made no explicit claim that this methodology would lead to a movement. The comprehensiveness of their approach, however, could easily give a reader that impression. For example, in a case study of an emerging movement, they described how they counseled the catalyst: "It wasn't a CPM [church-planting movement] yet but was getting close. As we listened, it was apparent that some elements of the T4T process were missing. We counselled him to incorporate the lessons from the next chapter."[7]

Steve Smith also described the person of the pioneer leader.[8] Based on multiple case studies of dozens of practitioners, Smith summed up the traits and competencies of effective catalysts this way: "Each of them possesses a healthy combination of a set of characteristics."[9] Most of those characteristics were verified by the empirical data of this book's research.

THE PLACE OF RIGHT MINISTRY METHOD IN STARTING MOVEMENTS

Building on the first insight that the right person is essential in catalyzing movements, we now add a second. The data of the research suggests that the effective catalyzing of movements is not tied to any one particular methodology. We asked effective catalysts what ministry approaches they used, and they indicated a wide variety of *nineteen* different ones. In order of frequency, the movement methodologies they use most commonly are:

1. Disciple-Making Movements (DMM) (mentioned by a wide margin) as described by David Watson[10]
2. Community Learning Centers as described by Victor John[11]
3. Church-Planting Movements (CPM) as described by David Garrison[12]
4. Training for Trainers (T4T) as described by Ying and Grace Kai[13]
5. Church Multiplication as described by George Patterson[14]
6. Focus on Fruit as described by Trevor Larsen[15]
7. Insider Ministry[16]
8. Zúme as described by Curtis Sergeant[17]
9. Four Fields as described by Nathan and Kari Shank[18]

It is therefore clear that different catalytic leaders employ different ministry approaches. However, we cannot say that just any method may lead to movement: All the movement-producing ministry approaches include *intentional multiplication* at their core. They also have the following principles in common: cultural contextualization, obedience-oriented discipleship, house churches, reproducibility, training of multipliers, and reproducible resources. Beyond these commonalities, the research does not support any claims that one specific ministry approach must be followed in order for a movement to take place.

Therefore, we can summarize the second insight as follows: All catalytic leaders use movement-conducive multiplicative ministry approaches.

THE RIGHT PERSON VERSUS THE RIGHT METHOD

Where does this leave us? Pioneer and apostolic leadership literature and movement publications have emphasized right methodology, with some attention to traits and competencies of the catalyst, particularly traits of a spiritual nature. However, the findings of this research go beyond the commonly established insights. The data clearly suggests that a particular methodology alone is far less significant in catalyzing movements than may have been previously assumed or documented—unless implemented by the *right person*. Three traits and competencies of a catalytic leader correlate directly with catalyzing a movement (explored in chapters four through six), while eighteen others show a strong association. In addition, three further factors (discussed in chapters seven through nine) also correlate with movement breakthrough. All three of these are internal factors, under the direct influence of the catalytic leader, who initiates, implements, and develops them. This means the catalytic leader and his or her competencies are key.

A few authors have presented this perspective before—most notably Neill Mims and Bill Smith, whose almost twenty years of research into movements led them to conclude: "At the end of the day, it is the man and woman of God and not the method that God blesses."[19] Movement thinker Dave Ferguson came to the same conclusion: "The greater the missional impact, the more obvious the pioneering apostolic leadership becomes."[20]

These authors confirm that the person of the catalyst, more than the method anyone employs, plays a most critical role in determining whether or not a movement will result. Bill Smith adds: "If someone says to me, give me the method or give me the curriculum, I know that they have not understood that this [the catalyzing of a movement] is accomplished through persons rather than methods."[21] *The right leader will develop and employ the right methodology.* A catalytic leader with traits such as radical learning and innovation, who also possesses the necessary socio-influential and transformational competencies, can find and implement the most effective methodology for the context in which he or she is operating. However a person who is trained to directly apply a certain methodology, but lacks the traits and competencies identified here, will be unable to implement it effectively.

This stands in stark contrast with many publications that emphasize methods and principles over the catalytic leader. I hope the findings of this research lead to a greater focus on the kind of person God uses to catalyze movements.

PRACTICAL BENEFITS FOR YOU

This description of a catalytic leader provides us with a personality profile and a competency model for aspiring movement catalysts. Every Christian ministry committed to catalyzing movements would benefit from considering its implications. For example, this profile can give helpful direction for

- mobilizing and screening new candidates.
- oversight and mentoring of movement practitioners.
- development of movement training. The most relevant traits and competencies can be selected for training programs and enable more precise formulation of learning objectives. This will lead to better training measures and higher quality training curricula.
- personal growth of aspiring movement catalysts. They can focus on traits and competencies in which they need to grow and identify specific learning objectives for themselves. These will serve as a roadmap toward becoming a more effective catalytic leader.

Movement breakthrough is not in our hands to achieve, but our personal growth is. The findings presented here show us what kind of person we can aspire to become, to maximize the possibility of God using us to catalyze a movement. Part five of this book explores next steps for growth.

Maximizing Your Chapter Takeaways

Recap

- The right person is essential for catalyzing a movement. Wherever you see a movement, you will find a catalyst with certain qualities.
- The most suitable method is also significant. All catalytic leaders use movement-conducive multiplicative ministry approaches.
- Only the right person is capable of tailoring the best methods for each unique context. Growing into the kind of person God is pleased to use should become our main pursuit.

Reconnect

Pause for a minute, connect again in your heart with the Father, and pray: *Father, please show me how you want me to live out what I've learned in this chapter, so I can align with your ways and partner with you more fully. Amen.*

Record

- The key insights God has given me in this chapter are:

Reflect More Deeply

Use the following self-coaching questions for prayerful personal or team reflection:

- Before reading this book, how did I view the relationship between the right method and the right person?
- How does the perspective that the catalytic leader's qualities are more significant than the use of the right methods fit into my ministry philosophy?
- How much do I prioritize growing into the kind of person God can use?
- How do I feel about the perspective that all the needed qualities for movement growth can be developed?

Realize

- I sense God nudging me to implement these key insights through the following action steps:
  - Action Step 1

  - Action Step 2

  - Action Step 3

PART FOUR

Movement Blockers

This section reveals the two most critical factors that block movement breakthrough. Both have shown to be negatively correlated with movements. These two factors are:

- People not being open to the gospel
- Limited time due to tentmaking or project work

Table IV.1 shows how pioneers rated these two factors, revealing a clear difference between effective catalysts and non-catalysts.

Table IV.1: The Correlating Factors Blocking Movement Breakthrough

Factors	Catalysts	Non-Catalysts	Difference
People not being open to the gospel	2.82	3.43	-0.61
Limited time due to tentmaking	2.59	3.07	-0.48

Chapters twelve and thirteen delve into these correlating factors, their role in blocking movement breakthrough, and how to address and mitigate them. In addition to these two blockers, chapter fourteen looks at other factors mentioned most frequently by practitioners as inhibiting or blocking movements.

Correlating Movement Blocker #1

LACK OF OPENNESS TO THE GOSPEL

There may be hardened people groups, but in every one there are harvestable individuals.

Steve Smith And Ying Kai

As you prayerfully engage with this chapter, you'll gain deeper understanding of the following topics:

- *The impact of receptivity:* Understand why receptivity contributes to movements, although not significantly.
- *Movements grow despite lack of spiritual receptivity:* Explore how movements can happen in societies with all degrees of openness, even those opposed to the gospel.
- *Receptive pockets:* Discover that every society has receptive pockets of 2.5 percent (or more) that are open to religious change.
- *Identifying receptive pockets:* Learn how you can develop a strategy with proven practical building blocks to find those who are open.

Before you begin reading this chapter, I encourage you to put the book down, pause, and pray. Connect in your heart with the Father, releasing to him anything that may keep you from being fully present.

Father, please show me what in this chapter you want me to learn and how you want me to grow, so I can align with your ways and partner with you more fully. Amen.

THE SIGNIFICANCE OF GOSPEL RECEPTIVITY TO CATALYZING A MOVEMENT

"How do I start a movement when people aren't open?" I hear this frustrated question more often than any other among practitioners seeking to start a movement. "I believe in movements. I apply all I've learned. But people here simply aren't open. What else can I do?"

Some have the privilege of sharing Jesus with people who are open to the good news, but many of us don't. Can a movement only happen among people who are receptive to the gospel? How does lack of openness affect the potential for movement breakthrough? What can we do when the people we are seeking to reach are just not open? These questions deserve thorough answers, and this chapter will give you some.

Our research compared effective catalytic leaders with other pioneers in the same context who had not catalyzed a movement. We asked both groups three questions to assess their people's receptivity:

1. On a scale of 1 ("not at all") to 5 ("very much"), how much did this factor (of people *not being open* to the gospel) *impede* the catalyzing of your movement?
2. How much did this factor (of people *being open* to the gospel) *contribute* to the catalyzing of your movement?
3. On the receptivity scale—called the Dayton Scale—how would you rate the overall receptivity of your people group to the good news at the time when you first took up residence among them? (-5 denotes strongly opposed, 0 denotes indifferent, and +5 denotes strongly favorable)?[1]

HOW MUCH DOES A LACK OF OPENNESS TO THE GOSPEL BLOCK MOVEMENTS?

Table 12.1 shows how catalysts and non-catalysts rated the factor of people not being open to the gospel.

Table 12.1: Lack of Openness to the Gospel as a Factor Blocking Movement Breakthrough

Factor	Catalysts	Non-Catalysts	Difference
People not open to the gospel	2.82	3.43	-0.61

Those who had not catalyzed a movement rated people's lack of openness as more of an impeding factor, with a score of 3.43, compared with the catalytic leaders' much lower score of 2.82. This constitutes the largest difference of all blocking factors between catalysts and non-catalysts. Lack of openness is a stronger inhibiting factor in non-movement situations than it is in contexts where a movement emerged. This difference reveals that lack of openness does hinder a movement.

HOW MUCH DOES OPENNESS TO THE GOSPEL BOOST A MOVEMENT?

Table 12.2 shows the rating pioneers gave to the factor of openness contributing to a movement. Their ratings were similar, whether they had catalyzed a movement or not.

Table 12.2: Openness to the Gospel as Factor Boosting Movement Breakthrough

Factor	Catalysts	Non-Catalysts	Difference
People open to the gospel	3.76	3.44	+0.32

Those who had catalyzed a movement rated the factor "openness to the gospel" second lowest on a list of ten contributing factors (3.76 on a 1–5 scale). Only one factor ("conversions without human involvement") ranked lower. Catalytic leaders don't see people's openness to the gospel making a significant contribution to their movement breakthrough. Non-catalysts assess it as making an even lower contribution (3.44) to their ministry fruitfulness. Openness to the gospel does not necessarily lead to a movement. It contributes, but according to catalytic leaders, not very significantly.

ASSESSING INITIAL RECEPTIVITY

As noted above, we also asked how respondents would rate the overall receptivity of their people group to the good news at the time when they first took up residence among them.

The assessment of catalytic leaders reflected their somewhat subjective perceptions. Remember, because these are effective movement catalysts, in every case, movements actually happened. Figure 12.1 presents what we found.

Eighteen percent of the people groups were assessed to have been strongly opposed (-5 and -4) and 34 percent somewhat opposed (-3 and -2). Fifteen percent were described as indifferent to the gospel (rated -1 to +1), while 19 percent were assessed as somewhat favorable (+2 and +3). Only 14 percent of all people groups were considered strongly favorable to the gospel when the catalytic leaders began their work among them.

In general, the leaders who didn't catalyze a movement rated the receptivity of their people groups as similar to those where a movement happened. The only noticeable difference is that non-catalysts assessed more of their people to be strongly opposed to the gospel (24 percent, compared with 14 percent for catalysts), rather than somewhat opposed (19 percent, compared with 29 percent for catalysts).

Where people groups had proved receptive to the gospel, the catalysts and non-catalysts showed very little difference. Among people groups where pioneers had not started a movement, 29 percent were assessed as receptive (somewhat or strongly favorable), compared with 33 percent of the people groups where movements had been started. Figure 12.1 shows the nearly even distribution.

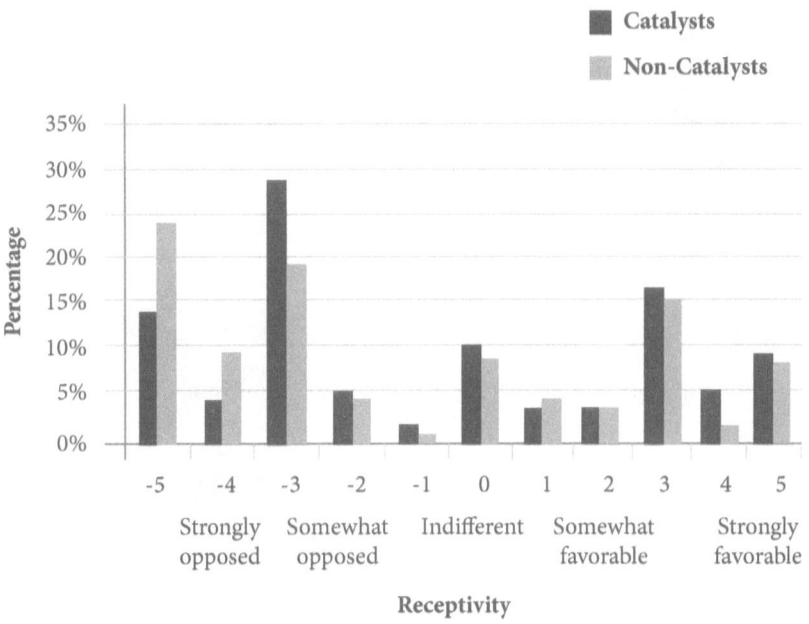

Figure 12.1: Receptivity of People Groups with Catalysts and Non-Catalysts

This demonstrates that the gospel receptivity of a people group is not a determining factor in the catalyzing of a movement. Movements happen irrespective of the overall receptivity of the people group. Movements can and do happen among people groups strongly opposed to the gospel.

In a different study, I asked catalytic leaders ministering among Muslims the same receptivity question.[2] Remarkably, slightly more movements had happened among Muslim people groups opposed to the gospel than among open people groups. Overall, the distribution was almost even. You can see this in figure 12.2, this time only for effective catalysts:

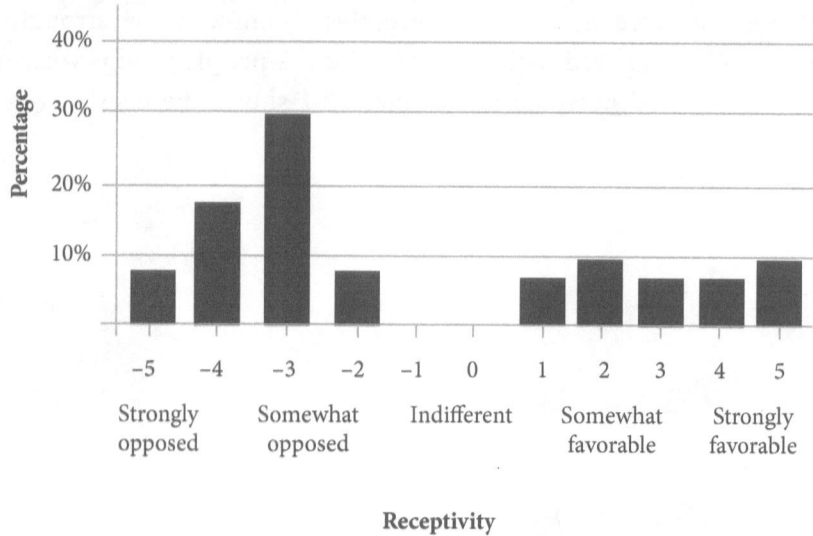

Figure 12.2: Receptivity of Muslim People Groups with Catalysts

KEY FINDINGS REGARDING OPENNESS OR
LACK OF OPENNESS TO THE GOSPEL

In summary, we see three realities:

- Lack of spiritual receptivity blocks movements.
- Receptivity boosts movements, although not significantly, according to catalytic leaders.
- Movements happen in societies with all levels of openness—even those strongly opposed to the gospel.

FRUITFUL RESPONSES CONCERNING GOSPEL RECEPTIVITY

What do these findings mean for your movement ministry practice? I suggest three useful responses, corresponding to the findings above.

Lack of spiritual receptivity blocks movements: We do not spend time sowing a lot of seed with individuals and groups in our community once we have assessed that they are—at least for the present—opposed to the gospel. This is what Jesus described as shaking off the dust from our feet (Matt. 10:14).

Receptivity contributes to movements, although not significantly, according to catalytic leaders: Because of this, we focus on individuals and groups in our community who seem to be open to the gospel. However, we do not assume that their openness will lead to a movement, unless we continue working to make our ministry reproducible and ensure consistent replication.

Movements happen in societies with all levels of openness, even in those strongly opposed to the gospel: If we are ministering in a society that is not open overall, we maintain the conviction that a movement can happen anyway. We take encouragement from examples of breakthroughs in other places irrespective of the overall people group's receptivity, and from the fact that at least 2.5 percent (see more on this below) will be receptive to spiritual change.

FINDING THE RECEPTIVE POCKETS THAT EXIST IN EVERY SOCIETY

Beyond my own studies, sociological research has observed that "at least 2½ percent of any society are open for religious change, no matter how resistant the whole society."[3] Data of movement practitioners worldwide provided to the ministry Media to Movements empirically verifies that this holds true for the growing number of societies where these practitioners do ministry.[4]

This means that if you live in a village of one thousand, you will likely have at least twenty-five neighbors who are open to the gospel at any time. If you live in a town with a population of ten thousand, you will have at least 250 individuals who are open. And if you reside in a city of a million, at least 25,000 of them are likely seeking the truth right now, whether you live in Miami, Mombasa, Mumbai, or Mecca.

The experience of seasoned catalysts confirms that receptive pockets exist within all societies, including those with a low level of overall receptivity. Steve Smith and Ying Kai's research into movements affirms this conclusion: "There may be hardened people groups, but in every one there are harvestable individuals."[5] Jerry Trousdale's research comes to a similar conclusion, pressing further to note that often "the hardest people yield the greatest results."[6] Trousdale observes the principle that "sometimes the most difficult person to reach with the gospel will become the most dedicated follower of Christ."[7] This observation does not refer to gospel receptivity among the entire people group, but to individuals and subgroups in society.

Once we embrace the conviction that receptive pockets exist in every society, how does this inform the way we do ministry practically? I propose a macro-strategy with a number of specific steps forward.

A MACRO-STRATEGY FOR A NON-RECEPTIVE SOCIETY

In my own ministry life, I have experienced the whole range—from hostility to openness to the gospel. In the capital of Sudan, I shared Jesus with Arabs who took pride in being Muslim and scorned anything Christian. ("Ah, you Christians cannot even agree among yourselves what you believe. Leave us alone! We possess the final revelation that God sent us after you Christians corrupted the truth.") In secular England where I currently live, most people are indifferent. ("It's nice that this works for you. I'm not very religious and don't need a god to have a happy and meaningful life.") In the people group where we saw a movement, people were disillusioned with Islam and open to a new paradigm. ("We love your Jesus stories; tell us more!")

Even though in each context I needed to relearn how to engage people in Jesus conversations, the general approach to starting a movement remains similar overall. Below are some practices that have proved to be essential in my own life and also in the lives of other catalytic leaders:

- **Live out a radiant spirituality:** David Watson calls this "conspicuous spirituality."[8] Live out a spirituality that is attractive and visible to all you encounter. Seek to:
    - be respected (especially in a status society) and likeable (especially in a secular society) as "a good person" according to the local value system.

- be known as an extraordinarily loving and caring person—someone others would turn to for help.
- become known as the "Jesus person" and a spiritual person to as many people as possible in your neighborhood and social networks—someone others with genuine spiritual questions would turn to. Many catalytic leaders do this primarily by being as warm-hearted and loving as possible.

- **Engage in wide personal gospel sowing:** Look for the 2.5 percent by sowing the gospel widely and indiscriminately through personal interactions. Catalytic leaders do this primarily through initiating gospel conversations using prepared statements of a spiritual nature that consistently turn everyday conversations into spiritual conversations. When you find someone who shows spiritual interest, drop everything else and love that person closer to Christ.

- **Engage in wider gospel sowing through media:** Use mass media and social media to look for the 2.5 percent through wider sowing. Although media messages are not useful for persuasion of non-receptive people, they help identify the 2.5 percent who are open to the gospel.[9] Using media helps to extend your influence beyond your personal networks, allowing you to access wider networks that could never be reached through personal sowing.

- **Guide the spiritually dissatisfied toward Christ in groups:** McGuire puts it beautifully: "The aberrant group [from mainstream society] finds their restlessness in the fact that the majority religion does not satisfy their soul. These groups are looking for someone to help them make sense of their restless soul. Helping the group as a group keeps the bonds tight and the vision alive."[10] These seekers are best led to Christ in groups of like-minded peers. Such groups form the basis for discovery groups and the nucleus of new churches.

- **Disciple the 2.5 percent:** Equip them to reach the next 2.5 percent, who will then be open. The first to respond to the gospel will be innovators, who need to be encouraged to become a gateway into their network of others who are spiritually dissatisfied and open to change.[11]

- **Continue to focus on finding the receptive pockets in your community:** Keep praying for those who are not receptive. Over time, you will move toward the center of society, until you have permeated it with the kingdom.

TAKING ON GOD'S PERSPECTIVE

In the city of Corinth, the movement catalyst St. Paul experienced a society that was not open to the gospel. People "opposed Paul and became abusive" (Acts 18:6 NIV). Paul was ready to quit and move on ... until God spoke to him in a dream and revealed his perspective: There are "many in this city who are my [God's] people" (Acts 18:10). Implication for ministry? "Do not be afraid; keep on speaking, do not be silent" (Acts 18:9 NIV). As a result, Paul continued his teaching ministry in Corinth for a year and a half, the second-longest of all his recorded stays in one place, and many came into the kingdom (Acts 18:8), even though, at first, Corinth looked like a society that wasn't open to the gospel.

Others' experiences are great, but I challenge you to seek God for your own personal revelation, similar to the way God spoke to the apostle Paul. Ask him to share with you his perspective on your community, to help you see it through his eyes and with his heart. Ask him to show you his plans for your community—to guide you to the 2.5 percent who are open to the gospel right now!

Maximizing Your Chapter Takeaways

Recap

- Lack of spiritual receptivity inhibits movements.
- Receptivity contributes to movements, although not significantly.
- Movements happen in societies with all levels of openness, even those strongly opposed to the gospel.

- Every society has receptive population pockets of 2.5 percent who are open to religious change. Finding them is key to starting a movement, and you can use proven practices to develop a strategy to find them.

Reconnect

Pause for a minute, connect again in your heart with the Father, and pray: *Father, please show me how you want me to live out what I've learned in this chapter, so I can align with your ways and partner with you more fully. Amen.*

Record

- The key insights God has given me in this chapter are:

Reflect More Deeply

Use the following self-coaching questions for prayerful personal or team reflection:

- **Living out a radiant spirituality:** How can we live out our spirituality more radiantly, more visibly, and more attractively?
- **Engaging in wide personal gospel sowing:** How much have we penetrated our social networks to identify those open to the gospel?
- **Engaging in wider gospel sowing through media:** Do we have a media strategy to identify those who are open to the gospel beyond our personal networks? If not, how could we implement one with the resources we have, even if on a small

scale initially? If so, how could we improve it and extend its reach? How many of the open 2.5 percent in our community have we identified?

- **Guiding the spiritually dissatisfied toward Christ in groups:** What are the social networks and groups of our seekers? How can we encourage seekers to share Christ immediately, even as they still journey toward Christ? How can we support them to introduce Bible discovery to their groups? How well are we guiding the spiritually dissatisfied in groups toward Christ?
- **Discipling the 2.5 percent:** How well are we following up with them? How well are we challenging them to become an instant gateway into their own networks?
- **Continuing to focus on finding the receptive pockets:** How can we continue to identify individuals or groups within our community who are receptive to the message? What does it look like to persevere in prayer for those who are not receptive?

Realize

- I sense God nudging me to implement these key insights through the following action steps:
  - ○ Action Step 1

  - ○ Action Step 2

  - ○ Action Step 3

13

Correlating Movement Blocker #2

BUSYNESS OF CATALYSTS

*Never confuse motion with progress. A rocking
horse keeps moving but makes no progress.*

Alfred A. Montapert

BUSY: Bound Under Satan's Yoke

Saying in the Indian Church

As you prayerfully engage with this chapter, you'll gain deeper understanding of the following topics:

- *Busyness is not a spiritual virtue:* Discover how busyness correlates negatively with movement breakthrough.
- *The place of tentmaking:*[1] Learn how you can identify a tentmaking role or compassion ministry conducive to your movement goals.
- *The root issues of busyness:* Look under the surface and find a disordered heart and a cluttered mind.

Before you begin reading this chapter, I encourage you to put the book down, pause, and pray. Connect in your heart with the Father, releasing to him anything that may keep you from being fully present.

Father, please show me what in this chapter you want me to learn and how you want me to grow, so I can align with your ways and partner with you more fully. Amen.

BUSYNESS—NOT A VIRTUE BUT A VICE

When Christian workers gather, they often talk about how busy they are and how much they have on their plates. For some, busyness stems from a tentmaking job or project work, at least partly. Such busyness can be viewed as a badge of honor—seemingly indicating a level of commitment to the Great Commission and to kingdom work. Being busy and talking about it can make a person feel important.

However, busyness is not the virtue many believe it to be. In fact, busyness is the second of two factors that correlate negatively with movement breakthrough. A catalytic leader's busyness often blocks a movement.

In this chapter I will describe how busyness can inhibit a movement. I will also share proven steps to move from busyness to fruitfulness.

UNDERSTANDING BUSYNESS IN THE BIG PICTURE

Busyness is not the same as working hard. By busyness I mean doing too many things—engaging in frantic activity that causes us to rush our work. When this happens, we lose the ability to be fully present to people, we skim through activities, and we neglect the most important matters.

Having limited time was reported as one of the two factors correlating negatively with movement breakthrough. Both effective catalysts and non-catalysts reported this as one of the two limiting factors, though less so for those who have been effective in catalyzing a movement. Whereas the previous blocker (people not being open to the gospel) is an external issue, having limited time is internal and therefore lies under the direct influence of the catalytic leader. This is good news: It can be mitigated. In order to do that, however, we first need to understand the proper place of tentmaking in movement ministry.

THE PLACE OF TENTMAKING IN MOVEMENT MINISTRY

"Tentmaking" can be either a requirement or a preference. Some catalytic leaders are bi-vocational and rely on generating income. Expatriate catalytic leaders residing in countries that don't issue missionary visas need a residence permit but also a credible identity to do movement ministry in the country. Other catalytic leaders do not need to do tentmaking work in order to reach the people on their hearts, though they may start a project to meet the holistic needs of the community and express the love of God in tangible ways. In less developed countries, these needs are usually physical or material; in affluent societies they are often psychological or social.

The first big step is to choose tentmaking work or a compassion ministry project most conducive to movement ministry. Tentmaking options are limited to some extent by the context, such as what jobs are available among the companies, NGOs, and ministries in the country. However, entrepreneurial catalytic leaders don't limit themselves by this factor. They simply establish a company, NGO, or ministry that contributes to their catalyzing of a movement. Although this can require significant investment of time and possibly finances, it can give much more freedom to make the best choices conducive to a movement.

From Experience: Eradicating Busyness

I have great empathy for everyone who struggles with limited time, with too much going on, and with feeling busy. I worked myself into burnout when I was leading a rapidly growing NGO serving more than two hundred thousand civil-war-affected displaced people. At the same time, hundreds of Muslims were coming into the kingdom.

Simply maintaining daily life in one of the least developed places on the planet required a lot of time, not to mention managing my team's safety in the midst of a civil war. Through that struggle, I learned to minimize the negative impact of the demands imposed on me by project work and managed to banish busyness from my life. I applied the same principles I am sharing here. It can be done!

A TOOL TO CHOOSE THE RIGHT TENTMAKING WORK

When determining what job or project will be most conducive to catalyzing a movement in your current situation, you may find it useful to consider the following three filtering questions. Drawing on Jim Collins's defining factors of great organizations,[2] our team determined that these criteria would guide us in choosing the right tentmaking projects:

1. What are the felt needs of the communities we want to reach?
2. Are we passionate about the potential project to address these felt needs?
3. Which project will give us the most hours of time spent with the people we want to reach?

We used this grid whenever a new need or project opportunity came before us, and whenever a new team member with professional skills useful in our compassion ministry joined us.

The reason behind each criterion is important.

Why meet the felt needs of the community? We bring the kingdom, we bring the love of God, and we want to demonstrate the gospel holistically. This is perceived most clearly by those we want to reach when we address their holistic felt needs. We identified those felt needs through focus-group discussions in the community.

Why is being passionate about a job or project important? We benefit from building into our lives as many things as possible that give energy, not drain it. God created each of us uniquely, loving certain kinds of work and not loving others.

Why choose the project that will give us the most hours of time spent with the people we are reaching? We have limited time, energy, and capacity. And we believe God for a movement. Therefore, we want to create as much contact time with our people as we can, allowing us to tangibly demonstrate love, model a Jesus lifestyle, and share Jesus with them.

ADDRESSING THE DEEPER ISSUES OF BUSYNESS

Limited time remains a reality for everyone. Even choosing the most conducive tentmaking work or compassion ministry project does not necessarily resolve that issue. A good choice turns tentmaking work into a movement ministry opportunity and reduces the problem of limited time—yet we all still have only twenty-four hours, only 1,440 minutes, in a day. A good number of these hours and minutes are taken by sleep, devotions, self-care, family and friends, and managing everyday life. We need to explore the following deeper issues.

Overcoming the "tyranny of the urgent."[3] In my coaching of movement catalysts, I have found that urgency often reigns supreme. When a catalytic leader tells me they are busy, I ask: "What are the main things keeping you busy?" In many cases their answer reveals their busyness is caused by responding to urgent issues that others bring to them. Effective catalytic leaders learn to discern between the urgent and the important. Steven Covey's four-quadrants time management tool—which categorizes task by urgency and importance—is an invaluable resource.[4] Focusing more on the "important but not urgent" tasks (quadrant two of Covey's model) is an essential skill for catalytic leaders. Always asking, "Is this truly important or merely urgent?" can serve as a powerful yet simple filter for anything that comes your way. I have adopted the practice of, whenever possible, praying over and sleeping on things before responding to a request on my time. By the next morning I usually have more clarity concerning how important something is (or isn't).

Addressing a disordered heart. When sensing someone struggles with busyness, another coaching question I frequently ask addresses a heart issue: "What drives you?" The answers that self-aware catalytic leaders give often point to a felt need for validation, which compels them to engage in activities to prove something to themselves and/or to others. They may feel a need for approval, recognition, meeting an inner standard, or meeting others' expectations.

The brutally honest answer for many leaders is: "When I'm busy, I feel important. When I am in high demand, I feel significant." The problem is, if we seek significance and value in what we do, we can never do enough, do it well enough, or impress others enough. Consequently, we do more: things that do not take us closer to movement. We land in a vicious cycle of continual busyness. This is less a matter of a disordered lifestyle than of a disordered heart.

An ordered heart wants most what God wants most. A disordered heart wants too many things, and thus easily loses sight of what God wants most. An ordered heart has a vertical and a horizontal dimension. The vertical dimension is our hunger for God himself that must run deeper than our hunger for a movement. The horizontal dimension, in our movement pursuit, is discerning what matters most now—what one thing we need to address now that takes us closer to movement.

Busyness renders us incapable of discerning and pursuing what matters most. A busy person has a disordered heart, therefore a cluttered mind. A busy catalytic leader cannot fully align their heart with God's. As a result, they cannot partner closely and co-labor with God toward a movement. Their busyness prevents a movement. Sadly, such busyness is endemic among Christian workers.

We must order our hearts. This happens in deep prayer, as we pause from our busyness, quiet our hearts before the Father, order our affections, and gain his perspective. Only then can we master our busyness and eradicate it from our lives. Only then can we deal with the tyranny of the urgent and set our feet steadily on the path toward a movement.

GROWTH PATH TO AN ORDERED HEART

When you feel busy or driven, pause and reflect on what is driving you. Identify spiritual motivators and affirm them.

- When you realize that your mind is cluttered, pause in God's presence. Reflect on where your heart is disordered, not centered on God, and drawn in different directions.

- When you realize that your heart is disordered, pause, direct your affections to God, center on him again, and ask him for his perspective.
- Regularly search your heart to make sure you desire God himself more than ministry success, including a movement.
- Regularly cultivate God's rest in your heart.
- Build the habit of weekly sabbath into your life—stop working, rest, and enjoy God's good gifts.
- Schedule regular breaks into your annual calendar. Block them out and protect them.
- Whenever needed, embrace your God-given limitations of energy, time, and capacity.

Maximizing Your Chapter Takeaways

Recap

- Busyness is not a spiritual virtue; it correlates negatively with movement breakthrough.
- Busyness can be mitigated by identifying a tentmaking role or compassion ministry conducive to your movement goals.
- Busyness can also be mitigated by addressing the root issues—the tyranny of the urgent and a disordered heart.

Reconnect

Pause for a minute, connect again in your heart with the Father, and pray: *Father, please show me how you want me to live out what I've learned in this chapter, so I can align with your ways and partner with you more fully. Amen.*

Record

- The key insights God has given me in this chapter are:

Reflect More Deeply

Use the following self-coaching questions for prayerful personal or team reflection.

If busyness is an issue for you, take some time out to reflect deeply on these self-coaching questions. If you are unable to do so right now, block out an hour or two in your day planner at a time that better suits your schedule.

- What are the main things that keep me busy?
- Among the things I am doing, which ones are not directly contributing to the vision God has given me (or my team or partners)?
- Where am I driven by the tyranny of the urgent? Where do I need to put first things first?
- What activities yield the greatest results?
- Do I need to change my current tentmaking role or the holistic project we run?
- Am I doing what only I can do (delegating the rest)?
- What among the things I am doing can I delegate to someone else, empowering them in the process?
- To whom am I giving my time? How much time do I devote to my key disciples?
- What drives me?
- How much do I cultivate God's rest in my heart?

- How much am I embracing my God-given limitations of energy, time, and capacity?
- How can I do less but better?

Realize

- I sense God nudging me to implement these key insights through the following action steps:
    o   Action Step 1

    o   Action Step 2

    o   Action Step 3

|4
—

ADDITIONAL MOVEMENT BLOCKERS

*Obstacles don't have to stop you. If you run into a
wall, don't turn around and give up. Figure out how
to climb it, go through it, or work around it.*

Michael Jordan

As you prayerfully engage with this chapter, you'll gain deeper understanding of the following topics:

- *Additional movement blockers:* In addition to the *correlating*
  blockers, discover the other factors catalysts assess to be most
  significant as inhibiting or blocking movements.
- *Internal blockers:* Six of the ten blockers are internal—they can
  be influenced by the catalysts themselves and their teams.
- *The mindset of catalysts:* Understand how an effective catalyst's
  mindset tends to be less concerned with hindrances than a
  non-catalyst's.

Before you begin reading this chapter, I encourage you to put the book
down, pause, and pray. Connect in your heart with the Father, releasing
to him anything that may keep you from being fully present.

*Father, please show me what in this chapter you want me to learn
and how you want me to grow, so I can align with your ways and partner
with you more fully. Amen.*

FACTORS BLOCKING MOVEMENTS

As noted on page 35, our team wanted to understand the *ministry factors*, other than the *qualities* of the catalyst, which significantly influence the emergence of a movement. Of the twenty-one factors identified, ten were identified as "blocking factors." We also categorized these factors as either "internal" or "external." Internal factors are those which can be influenced by the pioneers themselves and their teams, while external factors are those outside their immediate control, which cannot be influenced directly (other than through prayer). Of the ten blocking factors, we classified six as internal and four as external.

Figure 14.1 shows how significantly catalytic leaders assessed each factor to have *blocked* the catalyzing of movements. These are shown in

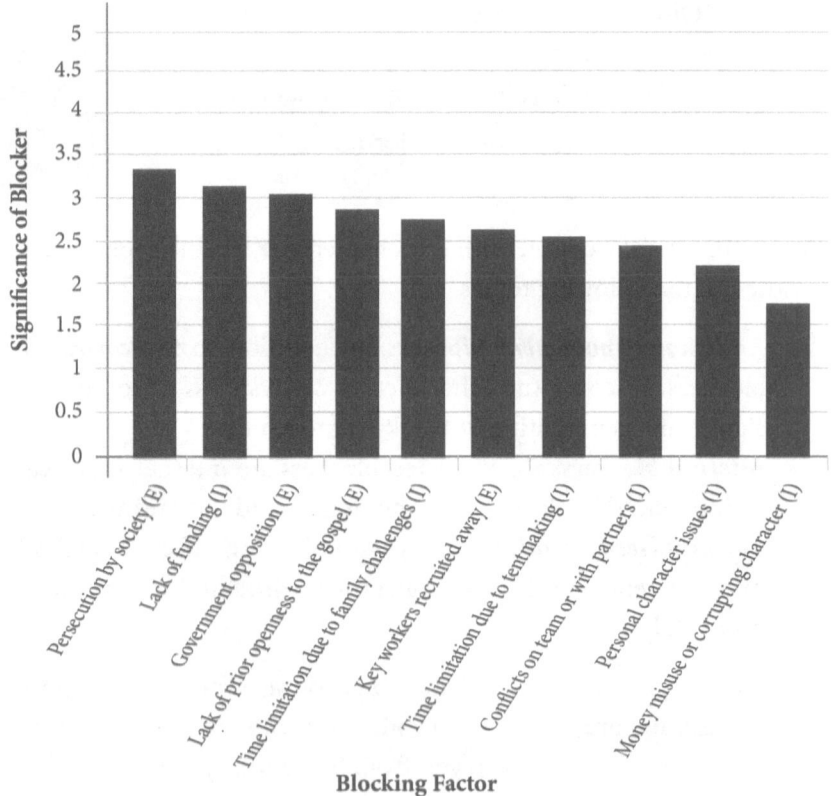

Figure 14.1: Factors Blocking the Catalyzing of
Movements, as Rated by Catalytic Leaders

descending order of impact. The "I" in parenthesis denotes an internal factor, the "E" an external one.

The internal blocking factors that catalytic leaders rated most highly are less impactful overall than the external ones (with one exception: lack of funding).

In figure 14.2, each front bar gives the average rating for the catalysts, with non-catalysts' average rating behind them. Figure 14.2 shows only the four factors for which the difference between catalysts and non-catalysts was statistically significant.

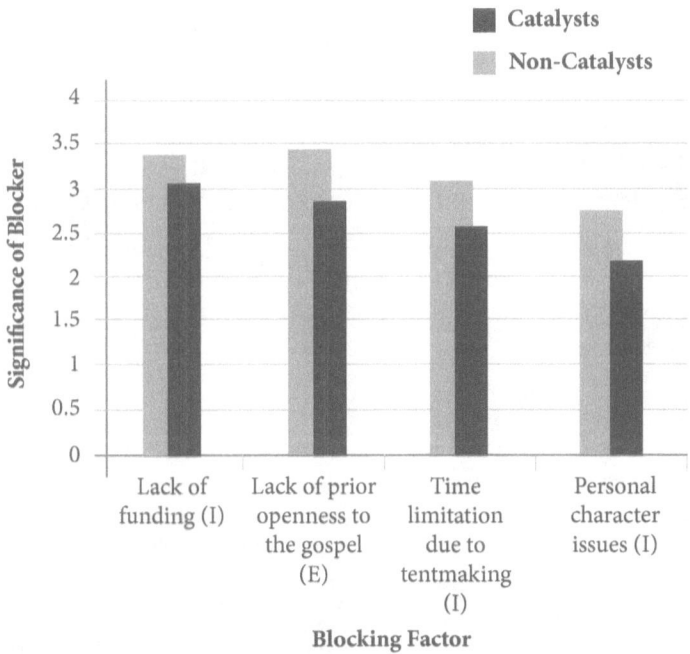

Figure 14.2: Statistically Significant Blocking Factors in Comparison

Note three observations about figure 14.2. First, three of the four blocking factors are *internal*: the practitioner has a great degree of control over them. Second, catalysts considered the only external inhibiting factor on this graph—"lack of prior openness to the gospel"—to be much less of an obstacle than did the non-catalysts (0.61 difference). Third, looking at figure 14.2 as a whole, we see clearly that non-catalysts consistently found these four factors more of a blocker than catalysts did. This suggests that an effective catalyst's mindset tends to be less concerned with hindrances than that of their peers' in the control group. An alternative interpretation is that catalysts faced lesser degrees of these four inhibiting factors than non-catalysts. However, since participants were chosen from the same or similar ministry contexts, the latter interpretation seems unlikely.

FURTHER FACTORS IDENTIFIED IN INTERVIEWS

During the in-depth interviews we conducted, we asked catalytic leaders the following open-ended question: "What main factors have *inhibited* the catalyzing of your movement? Please name the three most significant ones."

Their answers identified the following additional blocking factors, listed in order of the frequency mentioned, from most to least. They give us a fuller picture of blocking factors associated with movements, beyond those examined more thoroughly in the survey. Although useful, they carry less significance than the factors listed above.

Internal Blocking Factors

- disunity in church fellowship
- lack of finances
- character issues
- illnesses
- poor discipleship
- money issues
- lack of vision
- team disunity
- fear, shortage of workers
- lack of prayerfulness
- poor leader development
- lack of motivation
- pressures of daily life

External Blocking Factors

- other churches nearby
- occult spiritual opposition
- leaders poached
- illiteracy
- dependency on outsiders
- limited access to people group
- violence and conflict
- false teachings of other churches
- lack of commitment from local disciples
- lack of time
- lack of training
- other time constraints
- absence of Scriptures
- lack of meeting places

Maximizing Your Chapter Takeaways

Recap

- In addition to the two *correlating* movement blockers, practitioners identify other factors as blocking or inhibiting movements.
- Six of the ten blockers are internal—they can be influenced by the catalysts themselves and their teams.
- An effective catalyst's mindset tends to be less concerned with hindrances than a non-catalyst's.

Reconnect

Pause for a minute, connect again in your heart with the Father, and pray: *Father, please show me how you want me to live out what I've learned in this chapter, so I can align with your ways and partner with you more fully. Amen.*

Record

- The key insights God has given me in this chapter are:

- The questions I have for deeper reflection are:

Realize

- I sense God nudging me to implement these key insights through the following action steps:
    - Action Step 1

    - Action Step 2

    - Action Step 3

PART FIVE

Growing as a Catalytic Leader

The research underlying this book was never merely an academic exercise. The aim was to produce actionable findings and practical tools to empower you and your team to grow as catalytic leaders and to address the factors in your ministry that boost and block a movement. By understanding the principles and practices of catalytic leadership and assessing movemental factors, we can unlock the potential for kingdom movements.

The following chapters will explore the differences between catalytic and non-catalytic leaders, focusing on their approach to personal growth. Practical exercises will help you identify your blind spots and the areas most needing growth. By prioritizing personal growth and engaging in deliberate practice, you can develop the traits and competencies necessary to become an effective catalytic leader.

Additionally, these chapters will give you the tools to analyze your ministry context and identify the key areas that are boosting and blocking movements. This analysis will help you create an action plan to harness the factors boosting movements and overcome blockers that hinder your ability to catalyze one.

15

THE PERSONAL GROWTH OF EFFECTIVE CATALYSTS

Your leadership is determined by who you are.
John C. Maxwell

[People] are anxious to improve their circumstances, but are unwilling to improve themselves; they therefore remain bound.
James Allen

As you prayerfully engage with this chapter, you'll gain deeper understanding of the following topics:

- *Catalytic leaders' commitment to ongoing growth:* Discover that all effective catalysts are intentional about continuous learning and growth of key traits and competencies.
- *Non-catalytic leaders' lack of commitment to ongoing growth:* Learn that the personal growth of pioneers who do not catalyze movements tends to plateau or even decline.
- *The importance of deliberate practice:* Find out that the development of traits and competencies has little to do with ministry experience and more to do with intentional practice.

- ***Prioritizing personal growth:*** Explore how you can grow into the kind of person God is pleased to use to start movements.

Before you begin reading this chapter, I encourage you to put the book down, pause, and pray. Connect in your heart with the Father, releasing to him anything that may keep you from being fully present.

Father, please show me what in this chapter you want me to learn and how you want me to grow, so I can align with your ways and partner with you more fully. Amen.

OUTSTANDING LEADERS ARE BORN TO GREATNESS?

A widespread notion is that those in ministry either have leadership skills or they don't: Outstanding leaders are "born to greatness." Such conviction creates a limited incentive for both ministry organizations and individuals to intentionally invest in personal development. However, over the past fifty years, a myriad of studies in the field of leadership development has demonstrated that the traits and competencies of effective leaders are not exclusively innate; on the contrary, they can be significantly developed.[1] Unfortunately, this insight has not taken root among ministry workers. But if we are to see increasing ministry fruitfulness, we will need to understand how pioneer leaders can develop their leadership over time and find ways to support them in those efforts.

This chapter describes how effective pioneer leaders develop their key traits and competencies—with emphasis on the word "develop." We start by looking at the overall trajectory of the personal growth of effective catalysts over time, as compared to the growth of non-catalysts.

COMPARING THE TRAITS AND COMPETENCIES OF CATALYTIC AND NON-CATALYTIC LEADERS

My team wanted to know how catalytic traits and competencies developed over time and therefore analyzed the data against ministry longevity. Figure 15.1 shows trend lines of the average collective ratings for all traits and competencies combined, for both effective catalysts and non-catalysts, measured against years in ministry. (Again, traits and competencies were self-assessed, on a scale of 1–5.)

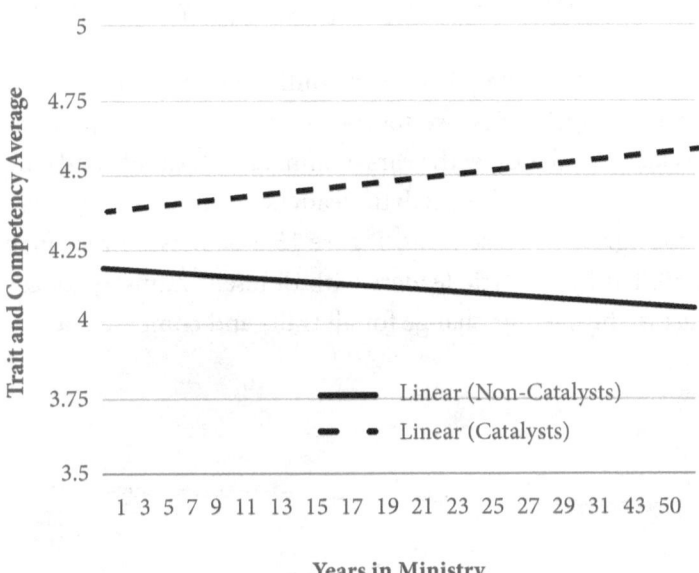

Figure 15.1: The Development of Traits and Competencies in Comparison

Four important inferences can be drawn from this graph. First, effective catalysts' capacity to start a movement does not correlate with their ministry longevity. Some start a movement after they have been in ministry for fifty years; others do so with very few years of ministry experience. Second, catalytic leaders start with an overall high level of the traits and competencies needed to catalyze a movement, and they continue to grow in these over their years in ministry. Third, non-catalysts, in comparison, begin their ministry with a similar but slightly lower level of traits and competencies, but then exhibit a tendency to decrease in these over their years in ministry. Both the increase and decrease are gradual and relatively small in size, but taken together they produce a fourth significant insight: Although the level of traits and competencies of effective catalysts and non-catalysts start out fairly similar, they follow opposite trajectories. Effective catalysts are set apart by an overall trend of ongoing personal development.

THE DEVELOPMENT OF EFFECTIVE CATALYTIC LEADERS

Although effective catalytic leaders continue in overall growth of their traits and competencies, we found two traits and competencies that have a clear correlation with years in ministry: flexibility and emotional stability. The longer the catalytic leaders continued in ministry, the more they grew in these areas. Figure 15.2 depicts how strongly both are exhibited by catalytic leaders with different ministry longevity, in contrast to the average change for all traits and competencies.

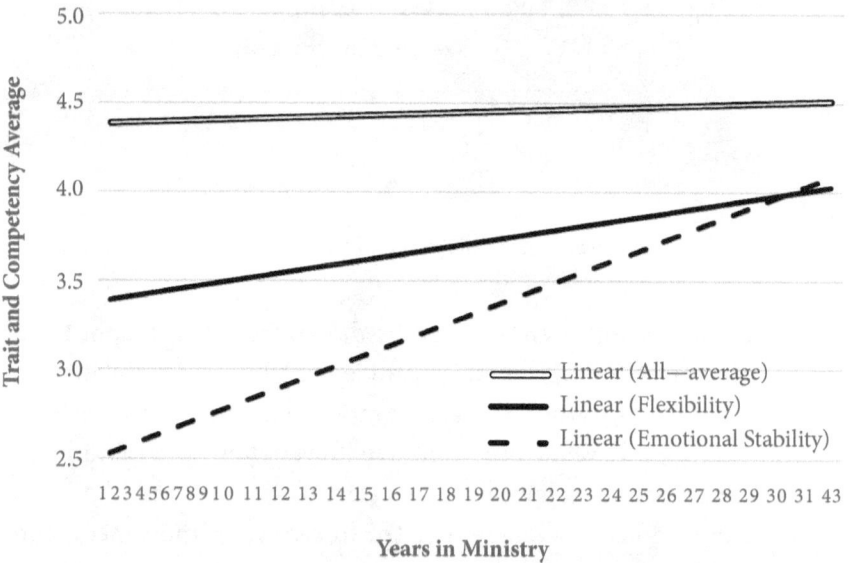

Figure 15.2: Trait and Competency Development of Catalysts

Flexibility refers to a person's willingness and ability to adapt to new situations, cope with change, and approach demands in novel ways, especially when stressors or unexpected events occur. Emotional stability indicates the ability to regulate one's emotions in ways helpful for interactions with others. Both flexibility and emotional stability are usually considered positive traits associated with personal maturity. For this reason, it is not surprising to see catalytic leaders' ratings of these two traits rising over their years of ministry. This represents growth in their personality, not in measures of behavior or proficiencies. This may imply that a major part of what separates effective catalysts from non-catalysts is the ability to grow and change at a deeper personal level, rather than simply a behavioral level.

The growth of catalytic leaders in these two traits is related to their overall growth. At an early ministry stage, emotional stability and flexibility had significantly lower scores than the other traits in the personality category—such as, for example, persistence or drive to achieve. The growth in these two traits gives evidence that catalytic leaders were able to correct a deficit in their personality. Although the increase in rating for emotional stability and flexibility was not large, it proved to be significant when considered over decades of ministry.

Next, we consider the striking fact that, for catalytic leaders, twenty-two out of the twenty-four examined traits and competencies have no significant correlation with increasing years in ministry. This finding provides fascinating insight into how catalytic leaders develop. Conventional wisdom would suggest that the longer pioneers remain in ministry, the more they grow and develop the traits and competencies needed for effectiveness. However, the stability of the vast majority of the catalytic leaders' traits and competencies over time suggests that ministry longevity alone is not a key factor in catalyzing a movement. Many of the traits and competencies related to starting movements are not limited to veteran workers.

This conclusion is confirmed by the varying ages of catalytic leaders at the time when they catalyzed a movement, ranging from twenty-one to seventy-six, with forty-four years the average age (both mean and median). These traits and competencies can be developed to a high degree irrespective of age or experience. This is supported by a wider review of competence theory in broader literature. Many studies have shown that the key to developing these traits and competencies is not time—in this case the years of ministry experience or age—but rather the amount of the leader's intentional effort to develop them. In sociology, this is known as "deliberate practice."[2]

FINDINGS FROM ALL PIONEERS COMBINED

Next, we look at the data as it concerns all pioneers, both effective catalysts and non-catalysts. This helps us isolate ways that pioneers in general change over years in ministry. Looking at the relationship between traits and competencies and length of years in ministry, we found that three traits or competencies showed a positive correlation, and six showed a negative one. In other words, the rating of three traits and competencies increased the longer a pioneer was in ministry, and three decreased over the same measure.

Traits and Competencies of All Pioneers that Increased

Looking at the three traits and competencies that increased in all pioneers (and having already examined emotional stability), we look now at persistence and empowering.

We defined persistence as the capacity to work with distant objects in view and remain tenacious in spite of challenges; to overcome obstacles and not give up amidst difficulties. It is not difficult to understand the relationship between persistence and longevity in ministry. All pioneers need to cultivate the ability to stand firm in their calling and overcome obstacles as they pursue a vision that is only seen by faith at the start.

Empowering is the other competency that increased over years in ministry for all leaders. We defined this as recognizing the gifts of others, enabling them to develop these gifts, assigning responsibility and authority to others (including the relinquishing of control and the risk of failure), and equipping them to carry out those responsibilities by means of mentoring, coaching, or training.

Traits and Competencies of all Pioneers that Decreased

Alongside the traits and competences that increased, others actually decreased among all pioneers with ministry longevity: assertiveness, evangelistic zeal, and disciple-making. Because these decreased over time for all leaders, their decline does not have a measurable impact on effectiveness in catalyzing a movement. However, it is still important to consider the reasons for this decline.

First, assertiveness: the ability to influence people and situations, even to the extent of dominating; sharing one's beliefs and convictions clearly so people take notice; and being bold and courageous even when facing opposition and threat. The decline in this quality could be attributed to a leader's attempts to soften the dominating side of their personality, thus rating themselves lower for this trait. As described in chapter six, the relation between assertiveness and effective leadership is curvilinear—too little assertiveness hampers effective leadership, but too much can undermine social relationships and thus hinder leadership outcomes. We can deduce that leaders who have spent many years in ministry have identified the right measure of assertiveness.

We now consider two qualities together: evangelistic zeal and transformational disciple-making. Our research defined evangelistic zeal as being driven by a passionate urgency to see the good news shared with all the lost, and passionately sharing it with everyone possible. Transformational disciple-making was defined as intentional Bible-centered teaching in the context of a transformational relationship that leads to heart obedience, encompassing spiritual disciplines and character transformation. The decline in these two traits is a natural consequence of the increase in empowering noted above.

This can best be understood by considering the statements we asked participants to rate for these two qualities. For evangelistic zeal, respondents had to rate (on a scale of 1–5) the statement, "I am highly motivated about sharing the gospel with others"; and for transformational disciple-making, "My disciples give me feedback that my discipling them has led to character formation and greater obedience to God." These both relate to personal ministry behaviors. The most likely explanation for the decrease in these two qualities is that the longer apostolic leaders stay in ministry, the more likely they are to focus on mentoring and developing local disciples while remaining in the background. Thus they would have rated themselves low on these statements at a personal, behavioral level. In fact, we might go so far as to say that a decrease in these traits and competencies could be a mark of a maturing pioneer leader because it demonstrates a focus on reproducibility in ministry.

THE CONTROL GROUP OF NON-CATALYSTS

The results for the control group—pioneers who did not catalyze a movement—provide the disconcerting finding that six of the twenty-four traits and competencies have a negative correlation with years in ministry. That is, the self-scoring of those who have not catalyzed a movement decreases for these six qualities the longer they have been on their field of ministry, as shown by figure 15.3.

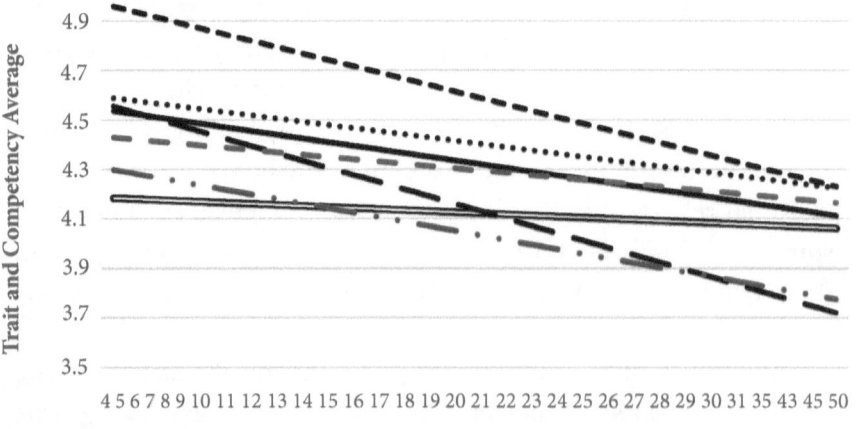

Figure 15.3: Trait and Competency Development of Non-Catalysts

The declines were slow but nevertheless evident. As three of the competencies showing a negative correlation to years in ministry have been presented already in the previous section (assertiveness, evangelistic zeal, and disciple-making), in this section we will consider the remaining three: agreeableness, expectant faith, and confidence in local disciples.

Agreeableness

The study defined agreeableness as a concern for social harmony that motivates individuals to seek out and maintain close social relationships, to be considerate, kind, generous, trusting and trustworthy, helpful, characterized by pleasant companionship, and willing to compromise one's own interests when interacting with others.

A decline in this quality could be viewed as part of the psychological changes that occur as people age, since some people become somewhat less agreeable as they struggle with the realities of aging. However, the data argues against such a generalized explanation because this score does not decrease among catalytic leaders. Only those pioneers who have not seen a movement are found to become less agreeable the longer they serve in ministry. Furthermore, the score for agreeableness does not decrease when measured against the variable of age of the respondent, only against years in ministry residence. This means it is specifically during the years spent in ministry that the non-catalysts become less agreeable. This likely reflects the larger issue of the way they handled disappointments, difficulties, and hardships of life. Although we can only speculate, it seems effective movement catalysts find a way to navigate the challenges of ministry without losing this winsome aspect of their character.

Expectant Faith and Confidence in Local Disciples

By expectant faith we mean the person exercises faith that God will show his power through their life, in particular that he will grow a movement and save many. We define confidence in local disciples as the confidence that God, by the efficacy of his Word and Spirit, will grow and use new and immature believers, and hence launch a local movement from local resources.

We will consider the decline of these two traits and competencies among non-catalysts together because, as it concerns movements, the second is an expression of the first. Faith in God may be an abstraction, but it becomes concrete for pioneers when they consider the fruit—or lack of fruit—in their ministry. In pioneer ministry, faith in God is closely connected to confidence that God really can grow a movement from local human resources. Thus, it is noteworthy that pioneers who have not catalyzed a movement become less and less confident as the years go by. It is impossible to say if one causes the other, but it may well become a vicious cycle.

Taken together, this leads to a painful observation: Over years in ministry, the traits and competencies of Christian workers can not only plateau but can even decline. Since the decrease occurs only in those who have not catalyzed a movement, it is safe to conclude that a key quality of the catalytic leaders is their capacity to maintain their cutting edge over years in ministry. Similar to a knife, repeated, prolonged use against hard surfaces tends to dull the edge. Therefore, its cutting edge must be maintained by repeated and intentional sharpening. Catalytic leaders stand out in their intentional efforts to hone their personal traits and competencies through lifelong learning and personal development. This fits well with our finding that effective catalysts are more radical learners than non-catalysts. (See table 3.2 in chapter three.)

SUMMARY AND CONCLUSIONS

Most traits and competencies of leaders (fifteen out of twenty-one) show no correlation at all with ministry longevity. This discovery has important—and encouraging—implications. Since most of the specific traits and competencies needed by kingdom pioneers are not directly related to development over years in the field of ministry, they are not in any way limited to seasoned leaders.

However, we found that catalytic leaders not only grow in a general sense, but they also demonstrate significant growth specifically in the traits of emotional stability and persistence. Catalytic leaders also become more empowering the longer they remain in ministry, which may be explained through a maturing ministry philosophy of equipping, as well as a growing competence in knowing how to empower effectively.

At the same time, sadly, some traits and competencies correlate negatively with increasing years in ministry. The traits and competencies of mission pioneers can not only plateau but can also decline over years in ministry. However, we note that the overall decrease in traits and competencies occurs only among those who have not catalyzed a movement. Therefore, we conclude that one quality of a catalytic leader is lifelong growth and learning, which translates into the capacity to maintain their cutting edge throughout their ministry.

These findings have significance for training and development. With only three exceptions, the development of relevant traits and competencies associated with catalyzing a movement does not correlate with length of time in ministry. This means that they also do not correlate with life maturity. We therefore see little correlation between the traits and competencies of a catalytic leader and ministry longevity.

This means any leader can develop to a high degree the traits and competencies necessary to catalyze a movement, irrespective of how long they have been in ministry. This fits with sociology's paradigm of deliberate practice, which has long held that the determining factor for high-level performance is not the amount of time passed but the amount of effort put into development. Effort here means a combination of training, mentoring, and the deliberate practice of the leader. What matters in enabling catalytic leaders is not their ministry experience but rather the amount of effort they put into intentionally developing their movement-relevant traits and competencies. Since all catalytic qualities can be developed to a significant extent, every movement practitioner should feel encouraged that they too can develop these qualities, even if they exhibit them only partially at present.

We are responsible for and in charge of our growth and development to become the kinds of people God can use. I hope these findings will spur you on to emphasize the development of your catalytic qualities and so improve your ability to partner with God in catalyzing a movement. The following chapters will help you identify areas for growth.

Maximizing Your Chapter Takeaways

Recap

- Effective catalysts have in common their ongoing growth of key traits and competencies.
- Non-catalysts' growth, in comparison, plateaus or even declines on average.
- The development of traits and competencies has little to do with ministry experience and more to do with deliberate practice.
- Prioritizing personal growth is essential in order to grow into the kind of person God is pleased to use to start movements.

Reconnect

Pause for a minute, connect again in your heart with the Father, and pray: *Father, please show me how you want me to live out what I've learned in this chapter, so I can align with your ways and partner with you more fully. Amen.*

Record

- The key insights God has given me in this chapter are:

Reflect More Deeply

Use the following self-coaching questions for prayerful personal or team reflection:

- Which of the findings in this chapter do I find challenging?
- Looking back over my years in ministry, how would I draw a graph of my personal growth in these key traits and competencies?
- How much of a priority has my personal growth in these areas been for me?
- How could I become more intentional to engage in deliberate practice and further my growth in these areas?

Realize

- I sense God nudging me to implement these key insights through the following action steps:
  - Action Step 1

  - Action Step 2

  - Action Step 3

16

A JOURNEY MAP FOR GROWTH

Pay close attention to your life *and your teaching; persevere in these things, for in doing this you will save both yourself and your hearers.*
St. Paul, 1 Timothy 4:16 CSB, emphasis added

As you prayerfully engage with this chapter, you'll gain deeper understanding of the following topics:

- *The importance of growth in the New Testament:* Discover the importance the New Testament places on taking responsibility for our personal growth.
- *Best practices:* Find out the three practices essential to personal growth.
- *Developing a growth plan:* Learn how you can create your personal growth plan to guide you in your intentional development.

Before you begin reading this chapter, I encourage you to put the book down, pause, and pray. Connect in your heart with the Father, releasing to him anything that may keep you from being fully present.

Father, please show me what in this chapter you want me to learn and how you want me to grow, so I can align with your ways and partner with you more fully. Amen.

TAKING RESPONSIBILITY FOR OUR GROWTH

Do you want to grow into a person God can use as a movement catalyst? This chapter will help you get there.

Let's recap. Wherever you see a movement, you will find a man or woman of God with a certain set of qualities. They may use slightly different movement ministry approaches, but they have the same personal qualities in common. It appears God is pleased to use a certain kind of person to start movements.

While methods matter, God always prioritizes the personal character of his servants. The right kind of person is required to work with the right methods.

Building the character of the catalytic leader ensures that he or she will be able to grow with the movement as it unfolds. And catalytic leaders are more likely to start a movement the more they grow.

This is good news in many ways! Many of the elements in catalyzing a movement depend on the catalyst, but a movement cannot be manufactured. It isn't human-made; it is "a divine-human cooperative."[1] Our part is to learn to cooperate ever more closely with God for kingdom multiplication. The more we move toward God, the more of him we have in our lives.

We are fully responsible for our own personal growth. God tells us to work out our own salvation with fear and trembling (Phil. 2:12). This is how Paul saw it—Paul, the catalytic leader *par excellence* and a key role model. Paul challenged those he mentored to make their personal growth a priority in their lives. Note the order in which Paul instructs Timothy: "Pay close attention to your life and your teaching; persevere in these things, for in doing this you will save both yourself and your hearers" (1 Tim. 4:16 CSB).

First, pay close attention to your own life. Second, pay close attention to your teaching ministry. Paul sets clear priorities: (1) your ongoing growth, then (2) your ministry.

Note the promise made to those who live with such priorities: "In doing this you will save both yourself and your hearers." Paying attention to your own life and growth will lead you to experience more and more wholeness, healing, and redemption. And it will lead to the same salvation and wholeness for those to whom you minister. Our personal growth will lead to the salvation of others. What a promise!

One key reason most Christian workers do not devote enough attention to their personal development is that many tend to see "gifting" as static. They've either received a particular gifting, or they haven't. Some are more gifted than others. Note the passive voice—"are gifted." It is quite telling. We often see "gifting" and "talent" as innate, whereas the New Testament clearly puts us in the driver's seat when it comes to our talents. In the parable of the entrusted talents, Jesus challenges us to steward our talents and make the most of them (Matt. 25:14–30). Paul urges us to "desire spiritual gifts" (1 Cor. 14:1), and to "fan into flame the gift of God, which is in you!" (2 Tim. 1:6). All catalytic qualities can be fanned into flame. They all can be developed further.

As we explored in the previous chapter, developmental psychology tells us that the main predictor of superior performance is not innate aptitude but deliberate practice: the amount of systematic effort put into the development of a skill.[2]

We also saw that the catalytic qualities of pioneers are far from static. They may plateau, which they do for too many Christian workers. They may also decline, which can happen with pioneers who never start a movement. And catalytic qualities can grow, as they do in effective catalysts.

BEST PRACTICES FOR PERSONAL GROWTH

The way forward is very simple yet very challenging:

1. **Prioritize your personal growth:** We need to develop the conviction that next to loving intimacy with God, personal growth matters more than anything else.
2. **Become intentional about your personal growth:** Growth will not simply happen; it will not just somehow evolve. It will happen as you take initiative, become proactive, and take practical steps.

3. **Systematically pursue your personal growth:** Our growth won't happen if we haphazardly turn our attention to it once in a while. But it will happen when we tackle it systematically and make a plan with specific goals and a regular rhythm.

HOW TO DEVELOP A PERSONAL GROWTH PLAN

The best way to be intentional and systematic is to create a personal growth plan and apply it consistently. Years ago, a well-known Christian leader challenged me to do this when he said he had yet to meet a great leader who does not work with a personal growth plan. Since that challenge, I have intentionally and systematically worked on my personal growth with a plan. Those who know me best say that next to the Father's affection in my life, this is the primary reason I have become who I am and have achieved what I have achieved.

Just as that leader challenged me, I challenge you. We make plans for the discipleship of others. We plan for all sorts of programs, even for events that are over in a day or two. Do we really want to work on our own personal growth without a plan?

To assist in developing a plan, here is a format with five simple steps that I have used in my Catalytic Leadership Accelerator with individual leaders and leadership teams.[3]

1. Seek support.
2. Discern your growth needs.
3. Set growth goals.
4. Commit to develop habits.
5. Evaluate your progress regularly.

Seek Support

Walking with someone else dramatically increases your chances of success. Very few reach their growth goals without support. Possible sources of support are:

- **Ministry leader**—who can mentor and/or coach, if he or she has a developmental mindset
- **Mentor**—who guides you toward growth in character and competence
- **Coach**—who asks insightful questions toward self-discovery
- **Spouse**—a sounding board, accountability partner, and/or cheerleader who offers unconditional support
- **Friend**—who may serve in any of these roles, depending on what he or she has to offer.

Ideally, a support person will also offer you regular accountability. If not, you need to find someone else. Research shows that sharing written growth goals with another person increases your success rate by 77 percent.[4]

Share your growth plan and agree on how frequently and in what form you'll communicate your progress—whether in writing, by phone, or face-to-face.

Discern Your Growth Needs

Assess your current level of the catalytic qualities. Go through the traits and competencies listed in table 3.5 at the end of chapter three and rate yourself on a scale from 1–5 for each of them, with 1 denoting "very little developed," and 5 denoting "very strongly developed."

In which two or three qualities do you rate yourself as strongest? Celebrate and be grateful for your strengths.

Which one or two qualities do you rate as the least developed? These will provide you with a good starting point to focus your personal growth.

Prayerfully reflect on the one or two qualities you feel most need to be developed. Use the following two key questions to help your discernment:

- **Motivation by desire:** Where do I sense the Holy Spirit stirring a desire for growth?

- **Motivation by need:** Where do I feel I have to grow, in order to meet the demands of my next steps toward a movement?

Ideally, invite feedback from those closest to you: your supervisor, peers, and those you lead.

Focus on one or at the most two qualities for maximum impact.

Set Growth Goals

Research shows that writing up your goals increases your success rate of achieving them by 42 percent, compared to just keeping them in your head.[5] Each growth goal should describe specifically what you want the catalytic quality (that you discerned as a growth need) to look like in your life. For qualitative goals, try to make them as SMART as possible: **s**pecific, **m**easurable, **a**chievable, **r**elevant, and **t**ime-bound.[6]

To give some tangible examples, below are some goals from my growth plan one year:

- *Hunger for God* **growth goal:** I want to spend more time every day consciously receiving the Father's loving gaze, which will deepen my hunger for him.
- *Tangible Love* **growth goal:** I want to make tangible love the focus of the way I relate to people so that they feel loved in every encounter.
- *Assertiveness* **growth goal:** I want to learn to apply the right measure of assertiveness so that I contribute to every situation that God gives me to add value, without holding back.

Commit to Develop Habits

In order to fulfill growth goals, you'll need to identify and commit to practical growth steps that will help you achieve your goals. The most effective way is to take growth steps that you can develop into lasting habits. Habits are the most powerful way to change. Helpful growth steps should be:

- Small and doable
- Concrete and specific
- Described with active verbs in the future tense: "I will do xyz …"
- Include a cue: "When doing x, I will do xyz …"

Again, to give some tangible examples, below are some excerpts from my personal growth plan:

- *Hunger for God* **habit:** In order to reach my growth goal (to spend more time every day consciously receiving the Father's loving gaze, which will deepen my hunger for him), I commit to developing the habit of taking a break after every forty-five-minute work block. During this time I will:
  - Release the encounter/work of the previous forty-five minutes to the Father.
  - Receive the Father's loving gaze.
  - Invite the Father into the next encounter/task.
- *Tangible Love* **habits:** In order to reach my growth goal (to make tangible love the focus of the way I relate to people so that they feel loved in every encounter), I commit to develop the following habits:
  - As soon as possible in an encounter, I will say something affirming.
  - When meeting someone, I will express physical touch, as much as culturally appropriate.
  - When being with someone, I will give them undivided attention and my full presence.
- *Assertiveness* **habits:** In order to reach my growth goal (to learn to apply the right measure of assertiveness so that I contribute to every situation that God gives me to add value, without holding back), I commit to develop the following habits:
  - I will experiment with being a little more assertive and evaluate the impact.
  - When sensing something intuitively, I will express my perspective or insight humbly yet freely.

○ When I encounter opposition, I will respond by saying: "Well, what if we look at it this way …?"

Evaluate your Progress Regularly

You may evaluate your progress by personal reflection; however, it helps most people to do this with their accountability partner.

The recommended frequency when beginning a growth plan—and in intense phases of life—is to evaluate your progress every other week. In order to create consistency and maintain momentum, it shouldn't be less than once a month.

In summary, as you seek to create a personal growth plan, aim for the following:

- Make it your primary ambition to become a man or woman of God who God can use as a movement catalyst.
- Develop a hunger for perpetual radical growth.
- Assess your strengths and areas needing development.
- Invite feedback from others: your spouse, friends, leader, mentor, coach, and team members.
- Focus your personal growth on one or two catalytic qualities.
- Set growth goals.
- Commit to create habits.
- Evaluate regularly.
- Keep growing.

Maximizing Your Chapter Takeaways

Recap

- The New Testament places great importance on taking responsibility for our personal growth.

- Three practices are essential to personal growth: prioritizing it, becoming intentional, and systematically pursuing it.
- Creating a personal growth plan is a powerful tool to guide you in your intentional development.

Reconnect

Pause for a minute, connect again in your heart with the Father, and pray: *Father, please show me how you want me to live out what I've learned in this chapter, so I can align with your ways and partner with you more fully. Amen.*

Record

- The key insights God has given me in this chapter are:

Reflect More Deeply

Use the following self-coaching questions for prayerful personal or team reflection:
- How consistently have I practiced the habits I committed to develop?
- Where have I made progress toward my growth goals?
- Where have I been struggling?
- What factors have kept me from following through more fully in developing my habits?
- Based on these insights, what I am committing to for the next period?

Realize

- I sense God nudging me to implement these key insights through the following action steps:
  - Action Step 1

  - Action Step 2

  - Action Step 3

17

ASSESSING THE BOOSTERS AND BLOCKERS IN YOUR MINISTRY

Remember—you can't beam through a force field. So, don't try it.
William Shatner

As you prayerfully engage with this chapter, you'll gain deeper understanding of the following topics:

- *The importance of understanding your force field:* Discover how evaluating the essential factors in your complex context helps provide clarity.
- *The value of regular assessments:* Learn how to assess the key factors that boost and block your ministry's growth into a movement.
- *Developing an action plan:* Based on the key factors you identified, use a practical step-by-step guide to develop your ministry action plan.

Before you begin reading this chapter, I encourage you to put the book down, pause, and pray. Connect in your heart with the Father, releasing to him anything that may keep you from being fully present.

Father, please show me what in this chapter you want me to learn and how you want me to grow, so I can align with your ways and partner with you more fully. Amen.

UNDERSTANDING THE FORCE FIELD OF BOOSTING AND BLOCKING FACTORS

Now that we have identified the importance of growing as a catalytic leader, it is time to do a comprehensive assessment of your ministry. This chapter will help you create a plan for harnessing the boosters and addressing the blockers on the way toward a movement.

Figure 17.1 visualizes your current ministry status and the factors at work:

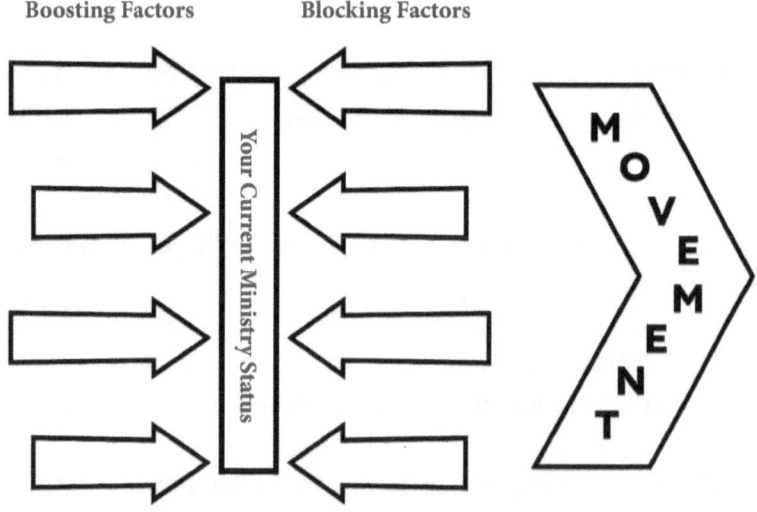

Figure 17.1: Factors as Force Field

From Experience: Assessing the Boosting and Blocking Factors

In my own movement ministry experience, our team regularly assessed the boosting and blocking factors we faced. In the early 2000s, before we had the findings of this book, we used what was available—Garrison's ten universal characteristics of movements—and we evaluated to what extent those characteristics were realized in our emerging movement.[1] For the characteristics least realized, we then determined one or two steps we would undertake to strengthen this element. One crucial moment came when we assessed our disciple-making and realized that, in order to have a more transformational effect on largely illiterate people, we would need to more effectively model discipleship—because emulation was our people's primary mode of learning. We decided to spend much more time in the villages sharing life with people. The results soon appeared. More of the disciples lived a Jesus-like lifestyle in everyday life.

At another point we identified lack of local leadership as a bottleneck to further growth of the movement. We therefore focused our efforts on raising up local leaders. As a result, more of the rapidly multiplying house churches had elders equipped with New Testament qualifications (see 1 Tim. 3:1–7 and Titus 1:6–9).

Since we did ministry in a volatile and hostile environment, we had to constantly monitor the external factors. Operating in the midst of a civil war and running an NGO that served more than 200,000 beneficiaries, we had to constantly navigate external pressures, so we didn't become too busy. Facing opposition from the Islamic government, we processed with the movement leaders how to deal with this challenge. The process equipped them to stand up for their faith courageously yet wisely. With persecution looming, we equipped local leaders to deal with resistance and outright persecution by taking them through New Testament passages about persecution. We always identified one or two factors that most affected movement growth, then prioritized addressing them.

ASSESSING THE BOOSTING AND BLOCKING FACTORS IN YOUR CURRENT MINISTRY SITUATION

Use table 17.1 below to appraise each factor of your ministry. Your assessment will yield the most reliable results if you do it with your team or partners.

Assess how strongly each factor has boosted your ministry fruitfulness, rating it on a scale from +1 to +10 (+1 denoting "not at all significantly," +5 denoting "moderately significantly," and +10 denoting "very significantly"). Make an X in the relevant box in the table. As you do this, focus on the actual contribution the factor has already made, not on what it might contribute theoretically.

Identify the factors with the *lowest* rating and circle them. These minimum contributing factors are your bottlenecks.

Table 17.1: Assessment Tool—Boosting Factors

Boosting Factor	+1	+2	+3	+4	+5	+6	+7	+8	+9	+10
Prior openness to the gospel										
Specific guidance from God										
Conversions without human involvement										
Prayer										
Effective ministry strategy or method										
Contextualized ministry approach										
Compassion ministry										
Signs and wonders										

Boosting Factor	+1	+2	+3	+4	+5	+6	+7	+8	+9	+10
Discovery approach/groups										
Reproducible disciple-making										
Effectively raised up leaders										

Similarly, address the blocking factors that you assess to have been hindering a movement in your ministry.

Using table 17.2, assess each factor of your ministry situation in terms of how strongly it has so far blocked a movement, rating it on a scale from -1 to -10 (-1 denoting "not at all significantly," -5 denoting "moderately significantly," and -10 denoting "very significantly").

Identify the factors with the *highest* rating and circle them. These are also bottlenecks.

Table 17.2: Assessment Tool—Blocking Factor

-10	-9	-8	-7	-6	-5	-4	-3	-2	-1	Blocking Factor
										Lack of prior openness to the gospel
										Government opposition
										Persecution by society
										Time limitation due to tentmaking
										Time limitation due to family challenges
										Conflicts on team or with partners

-10	-9	-8	-7	-6	-5	-4	-3	-2	-1	Blocking Factor
										Personal character issues
										Lack of funding
										Key workers recruited away
										Money misuse or corrupting character

CREATING AN ACTION PLAN TO ADDRESS YOUR BOTTLENECKS

Among the boosting factors, pick one bottleneck (one with a low rating) and develop ways to strengthen this factor. Develop an action plan with specific steps forward. At the end of the chapter, you will find a number of insightful coaching questions to help guide you. You can use table 17.3 for this process.

Table 17.3: Action Plan Development Tool for Boosting Factors

Boosting Factor	Rating	What We Could Do to Cultivate (Options)	What We Will Do To Cultivate (Commitments)

Among the blocking factors, pick one bottleneck (one with a high rating) and develop ways to mitigate this factor. Using table 17.4, develop an action plan with specific steps forward.

Table 17.4: Action Plan Development Tool for Blocking Factors

Blocking Factor	Rating	What We Could Do to Mitigate (Options)	What We Will Do to Mitigate (Commitments)

After you have carried out all the steps in your action plan, evaluate. Which activities have brought change? Which haven't? Continue to work on those that have brought about change.

Pick one other boosting factor that you assessed to be a bottleneck and develop an action plan with specific steps forward to strengthen this factor.

Pick one other blocking factor that you assessed to be a bottleneck and develop an action plan to mitigate this factor.

Work your way through the remaining factors, gradually strengthening the factors that will boost a movement and mitigating those that have blocked it.

Maximizing Your Chapter Takeaways

Recap

- Understanding your force field and evaluating the essential factors in your complex context helps provide clarity.
- In order to grow, it's important to evaluate your ministry by assessing the key factors that boost and block your ministry's growth into a movement.
- Based on the key factors you identified, the practical step-by-step guide can help you develop a ministry action plan.

Reconnect

Pause for a minute, connect again in your heart with the Father, and pray: *Father, please show me how you want me to live out what I've learned in this chapter, so I can align with your ways and partner with you more fully. Amen.*

Record

- The key insights God has given me in this chapter are:

Reflect More Deeply

Use the following self-coaching questions for prayerful personal or team reflection.

Assessing Current Realities

- Do we agree that addressing this factor is essential and timely? Where have we seen evidence for this lately?
- In two to three sentences, how would we describe in our own words what this factor looks like at the moment?
- If a boosting factor: What aspects of this factor are well developed already? What aspects need further development?
- If a blocking factor: What is at the core of this factor? What aspects do we need to embrace? What aspects can we influence?

Exploring Options

- In order to address the factor, what could be done? (Brainstorm several options.)
- What needs to be changed in the gatherings of the movement?
- What should the disciples change in their everyday lives? (Be as specific as possible about the change you want to see.)

Determining Action Steps

- Of all the options we have now listed, what are the few that will be most impactful?
- What are the action steps we are committing to before the Lord?
- Who will contribute to implementing these action steps?
- In which ministry situations (or challenges) can we take these action steps in the coming weeks?
- What will be the greatest challenges or obstacles that we will face as we take these action steps? How can we address and overcome them?

Strengthening Personal Commitment

- How motivated are we to take these steps? If needed, how can we deepen our motivation further?
- How confident are we that we will be able to do these things? If needed, what will increase our confidence?
- What support from others do we need in order to take these steps? Whom will we ask for that support? And when?
- To whom will we be accountable for these commitments? When will we tell them about this commitment?

Realize

- I sense God nudging me to implement these key insights through the following action steps:
  - Action Step 1

  - Action Step 2

  - Action Step 3

18

ESSENTIAL STEPS FORWARD

You don't have to see the whole staircase, just take the first step.
Martin Luther King Jr.

"Go slow to go fast." David Watson taught this counterintuitive principle for movement ministry. I've also found a related principle to be equally valuable: "Do less, focusing on the most essential." This highlights the importance or prioritization and focus over activity.

This book has shown ways effective movement catalysts partner with God for kingdom multiplication—and how you too can partner with God. In this summary chapter, I will highlight the movement essentials drawn from our findings.

MOVEMENT ESSENTIALS

- Cultivate deep hunger for God. Make sure your hunger for God runs deeper than your hunger for a movement. See chapters four and thirteen.
- Discern your potential role. Is God asking you to serve as primary movement catalyst, as a member of a catalytic team under the leadership of a catalytic leader, or as a movement servant adding value to one or more existing movements? Assessing your catalytic qualities, as described in chapter three, will help you gauge your ability to develop into a primary catalyst.
- Seek God for revelation of his plans with you and your team. See chapter four, especially the section "Marks of the Deep Prayer of Catalytic Leaders" on page 42.

- Building on this revelation, bolster expectant faith for a movement. Then pray and act with expectant faith. See chapter four, especially the section "A Growth Path to Deeper Prayer" on page 45.
- Assess the movement DNA of your current ministry, to focus on strengthening your minimum factors. See chapter seventeen.
- Among the ministry factors you strengthen, make sure you consider the ones that correlate most strongly with movement breakthrough:
  - Developing an effective ministry strategy—a strategy based on what God has shown you and addressing the felt needs of the people you aim to reach. See chapter seven.
  - Using the discovery-group approach. See chapter eight.
  - Effectively raising up leaders. See chapter nine.
  - Identifying the 2.5 percent receptive people and pockets if your community overall is not open to the gospel. See chapter twelve.
  - Overcoming busyness in your own life by ordering your heart and decluttering your mind. See chapter thirteen.
- Use the Catalyst Self-Assessment to determine your strengths and weaknesses as a catalytic leader. You can find it on www.catalyticleadership.info/assessment. Scan the QR code on the ad page at the back of this book for a $10 voucher.
- Develop a personal growth plan that enables you to grow intentionally into a person God can use as effective catalyst. See chapter sixteen.
- Among the catalytic qualities you intend to develop, make sure you include the ones that correlate most strongly with movement breakthrough:
  - Deep prayer. See chapter four.
  - Inspiring others' beliefs. See chapter five.
  - Assertiveness. See chapter six.
- Through training and mentoring, develop those in your sphere of responsibility in the catalytic qualities, equipping them to be catalytic leaders. See table 3.5 at the end of chapter three for a competence model of the catalytic qualities.

- Finally, review again the notes you recorded at the end of each chapter under the Record and Realize headings. Put them into action.

I pray that you will know how God is inviting you to partner with him toward kingdom multiplication. And that you will obey everything he is showing you.

If I can serve you on your journey, feel free to reach out to me personally at emanuel.prinz@gmx.net.

PART SIX

Frequently Asked Questions

In the preceding chapters, we have explored the various factors that contribute to the emergence and growth of movements. As we approach the conclusion of this book, it is essential to address two key questions that often arise. These frequently asked questions focus on the balance between divine sovereignty and human responsibility, as well as the role of miracles in catalyzing movements.

Chapter nineteen explores the intricate relationship between God's sovereignty and human responsibility in the context of movement ministry. It addresses the common tension practitioners face when trying to understand their role versus God's role in the success of their efforts, and especially in their stagnation. By examining the biblical foundation of the apostle Paul's perspective, this chapter provides insights into how to apply these two critical components appropriately: While we cannot control divine sovereignty or societal receptivity, the catalytic leader remains the key variable we can influence to drive movement success.

Miracles often play a role in the breakthrough of movements. Chapter twenty investigates how catalytic leaders perceive the importance of miracles compared to other factors. It also explores the correlation between deep prayer, expectant faith, and the occurrence of miracles. Through data analysis and real-life examples, this chapter sheds light on the impact of supernatural events in catalyzing movements and offers practical steps to cultivate faith and prayer for miracles.

These chapters aim to provide theological clarity and practical guidance for those seeking to start and sustain movements, emphasizing the importance of both divine intervention and human effort.

19

WHAT'S GOD'S JOB AND WHAT'S OURS IN MOVEMENTS?

The human factor will be the variable between
effective and ineffective church planting efforts.

Greg Livingstone

As you prayerfully engage with this chapter, you'll gain deeper understanding of the following topics:

- *The balance of God's sovereignty versus human responsibility:* Explore how God is 100 percent sovereign, yet we are 100 percent responsible for the outcomes of our ministry.
- *The responsibility of the catalyst:* Learn how our human responsibility as catalysts relates to God's sovereignty.
- *Heart postures:* Discover the important inner attitudes we need to foster in order to partner with God in movement ministry.

Before you begin reading this chapter, I encourage you to put the book down, pause, and pray. Connect in your heart with the Father, releasing to him anything that may keep you from being fully present.

Father, please show me what in this chapter you want me to learn and how you want me to grow, so I can align with your ways and partner with you more fully. Amen.

THE ROLE OF GOD IN MOVEMENT SUCCESS AND STAGNATION

While reading the previous chapters, I suspect some readers have thought, *What about God's role in all this? So far, you have only presented us with empirical data. We can't fully understand what catalyzes movements without bringing the sovereignty of God into the picture.* We now turn to this question.

Practitioners, wrestling with the tension of pursuing a movement but not yet seeing one emerge, often confuse their responsibility and God's. They may either over-emphasize God's intervention, neglecting their own responsibility for faithful action, or become overly focused on human effort, overlooking God's indispensable role in their labors.

I once spoke with a missionary who had labored for many years among a Muslim people group in Egypt, seeing next to no fruit. He recounted decades of efforts by his mission agency and his own outreach, all leaving virtually no impact in the Muslim community, expect perhaps for an improved reputation for Christians. He concluded: "Apparently, it hasn't been God's time yet for them to enter the kingdom. We trust that he has a plan for them." His report staggeringly lacked any evidence of an evaluation of their ministry efforts. There was no indication of significant adjustments to their strategies over all the years of fruitless outreach.

As with this missionary in Egypt, I often hear a similar explanation among practitioners when no movement has yet emerged: "God is sovereign." This conveys, "God's sovereignty, or God's plan, is the reason we're not seeing a movement here." However, that belief can become a self-fulfilling prophecy. Practitioners no longer have expectant faith for a movement. Their expectant "faith" now points to what they have accepted as God's sovereign plan: the status quo. And so the status quo persists. Essentially, these practitioners try to harmonize human responsibility and divine sovereignty by emphasizing the latter at the expense of the former.

Whatever one's theology—whether Calvinist, Arminian, a combination of the two, or any other theological framework—as Christians, we all grapple with the tension between two key realities: What is God's prerogative—which we must release to him and trust him for—and what is our responsibility?

When catalysts tell me the story of how their movement emerged, they invariably point to God. However, they do so to varying degrees. Some recount their story like this: "It was God from the beginning to the end. He prepared the hearts of the people we were reaching. Of course, we built relationships and shared Jesus. But he intervened, did signs and wonders, and transformed hearts. We just happened to be in the right place at the right time. I am not sure how much our contribution has been."

Others, while giving God credit, stress more the human aspect. They tell me their movement story more like this: "We labored for years, we ran compassion ministry, we loved people, we sowed loads of seeds wherever we went. Gradually, people began to trust our sincere intentions, see the harmony of our Christian community, and over time they began to see the beauty of the gospel. Initially we nudged only a few into the kingdom. But we poured our lives into those few and discipled them. We faced numerous setbacks. We had to persevere, and God gave us grace. But over time, one after another, people followed our example and became disciple-makers themselves. Then the movement took off."

Both stories point to both human effort and God's work. The emphasis, however, is very different. Ultimately, the difference in description doesn't greatly matter. The catalysts credit God, while also acknowledging how they partnered with him to start the movement.

THE THREE PREDICTORS OF MINISTRY IMPACT

I don't intend to present a comprehensive theology here, but I want to outline how the apostle and movement catalyst Paul understood and dealt with this tension. I call this a "minimal pragmatic theology" on the issue.

First, let us stake out a framework. Most theologians believe three basic components influence the emergence or impediment of movements.[1] I will describe each component briefly, then go to the New Testament and test how the apostle Paul viewed them and how they informed his outlook on ministry. Theologically speaking, these components are:

- The sovereignty of God
- Human responsibility of the recipients of the gospel
- Human responsibility of the gospel messenger

Most Christians believe in all three of these elements. Missiologically speaking, they can be expressed this way:

- God's sovereignty
- People's receptivity
- The catalytic leader (traits) and their ministry (competencies and methods)

Let's look at how these components affect the catalyzing of movements.

Essential Component #1: God's Sovereignty

The first component is the sovereignty of God. This is the belief that God determines all events ("all things"—Eph. 1:10) according to his perfect eternal will and plan. This component eludes all human understanding.[2] The apostle Paul conveys this elusiveness when, after expounding on God's sovereignty in Romans 9–11, he writes: "How unsearchable are his judgments and how inscrutable his ways!" (Rom. 11:33). We can't fully comprehend or accurately discern all God's ways.

It is equally true that human beings are responsible for their every action, and human decisions are genuine decisions, which have a real impact on the outcome of events (Josh. 24:14–20).[3] This human responsibility applies both to people who hear the gospel and to the catalysts who share the gospel with them.

Essential Component #2: People's Receptivity

The second component in effectively catalyzing a movement is the receptivity of the individuals among whom the good news is spread. Those outside the kingdom are responsible for whether or not they resist the good news (Acts 7:51) and for whether or not they repent (Acts 17:30). Jesus teaches that the amount of fruit may not lie in the effort of the sower but in the fertility of the soil (see Matt. 13:23). Examples in today's missions contexts appear to confirm this. Some people groups and regions show great receptivity, where almost every church-planting team sees fruit. Examples include Albanians and Kabyle Berbers in North Africa.[4] Other people groups' receptivity is so low that teams have seen hardly any fruit at all, even as they have implanted the gospel into communities—for example among the Malay or Bruneians.[5]

Essential Component #3: The Catalytic Leader and Their Ministry

The third component in effectively catalyzing a movement is the person of the catalytic leader—their traits and ministry competencies and methods. This component is grounded in the biblical teaching on human responsibility, which theologian Wayne Grudem defines thus: "God has made us responsible for our actions, which have real and eternally significant results" and do "change the course of events."[6] Since God has chosen to use human agents to take the good news of his kingdom to humanity, the conviction that the disciple carries full responsibility for their ministry applies to movement catalyzing as well.

HOW PAUL VIEWED THE GOD COMPONENT AND HUMAN COMPONENTS IN MINISTRY

Having formulated these three theological convictions, let us now look at the New Testament to help us apply them in greater detail. We will test them by considering how the apostle Paul viewed them in his movement ministry. Paul's sequential chain in Romans 10:13–15 indicates the critical component of the catalytic leader. This chain (and I simply reverse Paul's order) must occur before a person comes to faith in the gospel:

1. God sends a "sent one" (the meaning of ἀπόστολος [apostle or missionary])—v. 15.[7]
2. The sent one preaches—vv. 14–15.
3. Unbelievers hear—v. 14.
4. Unbelievers believe—v. 14.
5. Unbelievers, having become believers, call on the name of the Lord—v. 13.
6. They are saved—v. 13.

This chain of events can be summarized in the rhetorical question: "How can they call on the Lord without the 'sent one'—the catalytic leader?" They cannot! The person and ministry of the catalytic leader constitute an essential element.

In 1 Corinthians 3:10–15 Paul frames how he views his human responsibility. He describes the care taken in his own efforts, stating, "Like a skilled master builder I laid a foundation" (v. 10). His comparison of himself to a "skilled master builder" refers explicitly to his skills. Note that skills do significantly impact the outcome: "The fire will test what sort of work each one has done" (v. 13). The Greek word ὁποῖόν, here translated as "what sort," means "quality or manner." In other words, the quality of the catalytic leader's ministry determines the outcomes: the results either survive or are burned up (vv. 14–15).[8] Paul's ministry can be considered similar in nature to that of a modern-day catalyst. Accordingly, a catalytic leader's "quality of work" determines whether or not it will last.

Paul succinctly summarizes this confluence of the divine and human components in the same paragraph, when referring to those who build God's church as "God's fellow workers" (1 Cor. 3:9). The

Greek word he uses for fellow workers is συνεργοί, the root from which our English word "synergy" is derived. The effective catalyzing of a movement is the synergy of the human component with the divine. David Garrison calls it "a divine-human cooperative."[9]

These biblical foundations from Paul confirm that while he is certainly aware of God's sovereignty (Essential Component #1), and considers the receptivity of people (Essential Component #2), he greatly emphasizes the critical role of the catalytic leader (Essential Component #3).

Paul embraces this tension: God is sovereign, and humans are responsible. His choice of words in these verses reflects his conviction that God is 100 percent sovereign, and we are 100 percent responsible. Paul doesn't remove even 1 percent of our responsibility as gospel messengers. Rather, he highlights the skills of the master builder and the quality of each builder's work.

BALANCING DIVINE SOVEREIGNTY AND HUMAN RESPONSIBILITY

Charles Haddon Spurgeon, the great nineteenth-century preacher, compares the doctrines of God's sovereignty and human responsibility to two parallel lines that we cannot—and must not—bring together.

> That God predestines, and yet that man is responsible, are two facts that few can see clearly. They are believed to be inconsistent or contradictory to each other.... They are two lines that are so neatly parallel, that the human mind which pursues them farthest will never discover that they converge, but they do converge, and they will meet somewhere in eternity, close to the throne of God, whence all truth doth spring.[10]

Spurgeon points out that these convictions don't fit with Aristotelian logic, which says it must be either/or but cannot be both. Only in eternity, before the throne of God, will these doctrines make complete sense to us. Spurgeon also urges us not to attempt to reconcile both truths: "These two truths, I do not believe, can ever be welded into one upon any human anvil, but one they shall be in eternity."[11]

This is well-illustrated by the following counsel, attributed to Martin Luther: "When you are in a small vessel on open water and caught up in a storm, pray as if rowing doesn't help. And row as if praying doesn't help." In other words, Trust God because 100 percent depends on God. At the same time, you must fulfil your human responsibility because 100 percent depends on it. Applying Luther's teaching to movement ministry, we might say: "Pursue movement ministry as if all depended on your responsibility. Put your trust in God through prayer as if all depended on God.

THE THREE REASONS MOVEMENTS HAPPEN

Combined, yet still distinct, these three convictions mean that the following propositions are equally true, and need to be held next to each other as "straight lines":

- Wherever people come to faith in Jesus Christ, it is because of God's sovereign choice. Wherever a movement emerges, God has sovereignly willed for it to happen.
- Where the good news has been proclaimed in meaningful ways, individuals make a genuine, volitional decision to accept or reject Jesus Christ, a decision for which they will be held responsible. Where the good news has been proclaimed in meaningful ways and a movement has not happened, one reason is that individuals have willfully rejected it.[12]
- Each catalytic leader makes genuine decisions as to how to live their life and carry out their ministry within their focus community. These decisions can be conducive to the catalyzing of a movement, or they can hinder it. Wherever a movement occurs, it is because a catalytic leader has labored as a wise master builder.

Figure 19.1 depicts the three propositions. The clouds indicate that this component transcends our analysis:

God's Sovereignty

Recipient's Receptivity   Catalyst's Qualities

Figure 19.1: The God and Human Component Triangle

THE CRITICAL COMPONENT: THE CATALYTIC LEADER

While holding these three biblical convictions to be equally true, on a practical level the catalytic leader is a critical human component in whether or not a movement emerges. Note that in this discussion, with the exception of Luther, I quote exclusively Calvinist theologians. This is not because they reflect my theology but to demonstrate that even theologians who strongly emphasize God's sovereignty also stress human responsibility. We have seen (in chapter twelve) that movements happen irrespective of the receptivity of society, both among people groups open to the good news and people strongly opposed to it. This suggests that the "receptivity" component is less significant in movement catalyzing than the "catalytic leader" component. The weight of the data tips the scale toward the role of catalytic leaders. We have also seen (in chapter three) that the catalytic leaders' qualities are essential, and that God uses catalytic leaders with a certain set of traits and competencies. Among the three essential components, only our own life is directly within our influence.

Paul states that the quality of ministry produces certain ministry outcomes (1 Cor. 3:13). He also points out that modeling is absolutely essential in Christian discipleship (2 Tim. 3:10).

Therefore, a catalytic leader's traits will influence their effectiveness. The catalytic leader's skills and competencies, which Paul mentions in 1 Corinthians 3:10, will also influence their effectiveness. Social sciences have concurred with these biblical insights on social influence. They posit that we teach what we know, but we reproduce who we are. This all places more weight on the catalyst components than on others in our analysis. Figure 19.2 depicts the uneven distribution of significance:

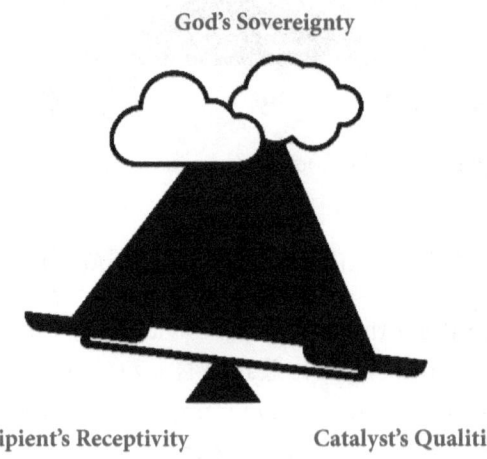

Figure 19.2: The God and Human Component Triangle (Weighted)

Greg Livingstone, himself a strong believer in God's sovereignty, aptly summarizes the importance of the human component in his doctoral study on Muslim ministry: "The human factor will be the variable between effective and ineffective church planting efforts."[13]

The biblical foundation from the apostle Paul and the data from movements worldwide points to the same conclusion: The human component of the catalytic leader is the key variable within our grasp, distinguishing ministry that produces a movement from that which does not.

A GROWTH PATH FOR HOLDING ALL THREE COMPONENTS TOGETHER

When we apply this conviction to practical movement ministry, we can assume the following postures, which enable us to follow Paul's example. We must:

- heed Paul's admonition that God's sovereignty is "unsearchable" and "inscrutable" (Rom. 11:33) and not attempt to blithely explain the absence of a movement with God's sovereignty;
- do ministry in collaboration and synergy with God, partnering with him closely (1 Cor. 3:9); and
- focus our attention on our responsibility and continually evaluate "the quality of [our] work" (1 Cor. 3:13).

Maximizing Your Chapter Takeaways

Recap

- God is 100 percent sovereign, yet we are 100 percent responsible for the outcomes of our ministry.
- We should not explain the absence of a movement with God's sovereignty, as his sovereignty is inscrutable.
- We need to focus 100 percent on our human responsibility, partner closely with God, and continually evaluate the quality of our work toward kingdom multiplication.

Reconnect

Pause for a minute, connect again in your heart with the Father, and pray: *Father, please show me how you want me to live out what I've learned in this chapter, so I can align with your ways and partner with you more fully. Amen.*

Record

- The key insights God has given me in this chapter are:

- The questions I have for deeper reflection are:

Reflect More Deeply

Use the following self-coaching questions for prayerful personal or team reflection:

- How much weight do I attribute to each of the three components as a reason our ministry has or has not seen a movement?
- How much have I seen the knee-jerk reaction in myself or my team that absence of fruit "must be God's plan" or "is due to God's sovereignty"?
- How can my team and I collaborate more closely with God, conducting our ministry based on the things he has spoken to us?
- How regularly and deeply do we evaluate the quality of our ministry, aiming for lasting impact?

Realize

- I sense God nudging me to implement these key insights through the following action steps:
    - Action Step 1

    - Action Step 2

    - Action Step 3

20

WHAT ROLE DO MIRACLES PLAY IN MOVEMENT BREAKTHROUGH?

God can work through the natural, but His supernatural nature often breaks through in miraculous ways.

Unknown

As you prayerfully engage with this chapter, you'll gain deeper understanding of the following topics:

- *How significantly miracles contribute to movements:* Learn how catalytic leaders assess the significance of this factor compared to other factors that contributed to their movement.
- *The link between deep prayer and faith with miracles:* Discover the correlation of catalytic leaders' expectant faith and deep prayer life with the occurrence of miracles in their ministries.

Before you begin reading this chapter, I encourage you to put the book down, pause, and pray. Connect in your heart with the Father, releasing to him anything that may keep you from being fully present.

Father, please show me what in this chapter you want me to learn and how you want me to grow, so I can align with your ways and partner with you more fully. Amen.

THE IMPACT OF MIRACLES ON MOVEMENT BREAKTHROUGH

The movements happening around the world today are extraordinary phenomena, many of which are characterized by miracles, signs, and wonders. Our survey asked catalytic leaders, "To what extent have signs and wonders accompanying proclamation contributed to the catalyzing of your movement?" Figure 20.1 displays the answers to this question.

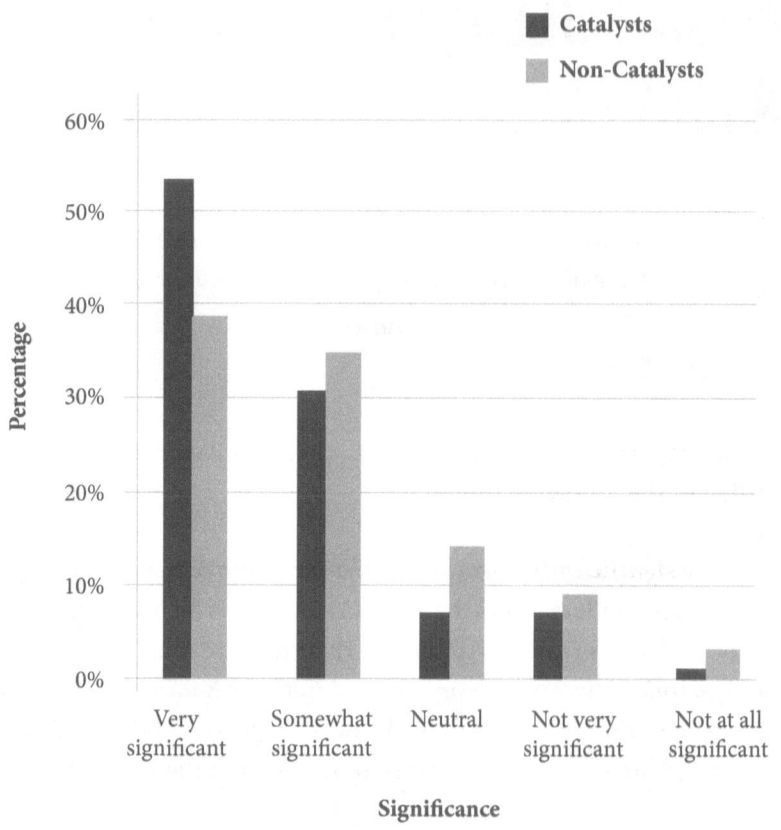

Figure 20.1: How Miracles Contribute to Movements

Overall, signs and wonders contribute significantly to movements; 54 percent of catalytic leaders surveyed said they contributed very significantly. More than five times as many catalytic leaders considered signs and wonders "somewhat significant" or "very significant" as compared to the number who saw them as "neutral," "not at all significant," or "not very significant."

However, we must be careful not to overstate their importance. Fifteen percent of the catalytic leaders saw movements happen without miracles playing a significant role. When the study compared the impact of miracles with ten other factors contributing to catalyzing a movement, this was one of the less significant ones, with only four factors rating lower. So, miraculous phenomena are not a universal prerequisite for movements; however, they do carry notable weight.

EXAMPLES OF SIGNS AND WONDERS

To add a qualitative dimension to the statistical analysis of data, here are some of the actual experiences of pioneers. What kind of signs and wonders did they witness? What was the impact on the people they were seeking to reach?

A catalyst from South Asia described supernatural acts of healing and deliverance as a normal part of his ministry:

> Deliverance ministry and other answered prayers have a big impact in a village. Most villages are filled with evil spirits … all families have issues—whether sickness, marital conflict, problems with the children, unemployment, or whatever. They tell us their problems, and we pray for them. It's just a simple prayer that can affect these people … and because they have seen miracles, they bring along others too.

A catalyst from Southeast Asia reported how miracles led to massive growth of new house churches:

> I think we went from about two hundred to 1,500 house churches within a period of three years after we started to preach and teach on healing. Now we have a movement of people who—mostly the women—love to lay hands on the sick and anoint people with coconut oil.

Some of the supernatural events involve power encounters, as this South Asian catalyst's story shows:

I've been in a village where all the dogs from the village just came charging at me. A crowd of people—maybe fifty to sixty or a hundred people—were standing there, and they were wondering, *What's going on here?* All the street dogs were about to bite … and I just took the authority. I looked at the dogs and said, "In Jesus' name, I command you to go!" The dogs turned and went away, with all those people watching. Inside, of course, you are scared, but outside you have to recognize who you represent because you are in Christ.

A pioneer in Latin America had the opposite experience when his horse knew better than he did, and it saved his life:

I was riding my horse to go to a meeting in another village. The miracle was that my horse refused to go on that road I was supposed to go on! I had to take another, roundabout route. After I got to that village, I learned that a group of men with guns had been waiting to kill me and stop me entering the village—but God saved me.

Sometimes the pioneers themselves were taken by surprise when God used them in supernatural ways. A church planter in East Asia, whose denomination was (as he put it) "not into signs and wonders," told this story:

A man invited us to his house, and we were talking until about 2 a.m. His mother was sick in bed, with an IV drip hooked up to her.… I laid hands on her and prayed, and as I did so I felt a heat coming from my hands.… At breakfast the next morning, this old woman who had been bedridden was there helping to cook the breakfast!

IMPACT OF CONVERSIONS WITHOUT HUMAN INVOLVEMENT

We also asked catalytic leaders a more specific but related question: "To what extent have you experienced conversions without human involvement contributing to your fruit, for example Jesus appearing to people in dreams or visions, or people coming to faith by reading the Bible without any human agent involved?"

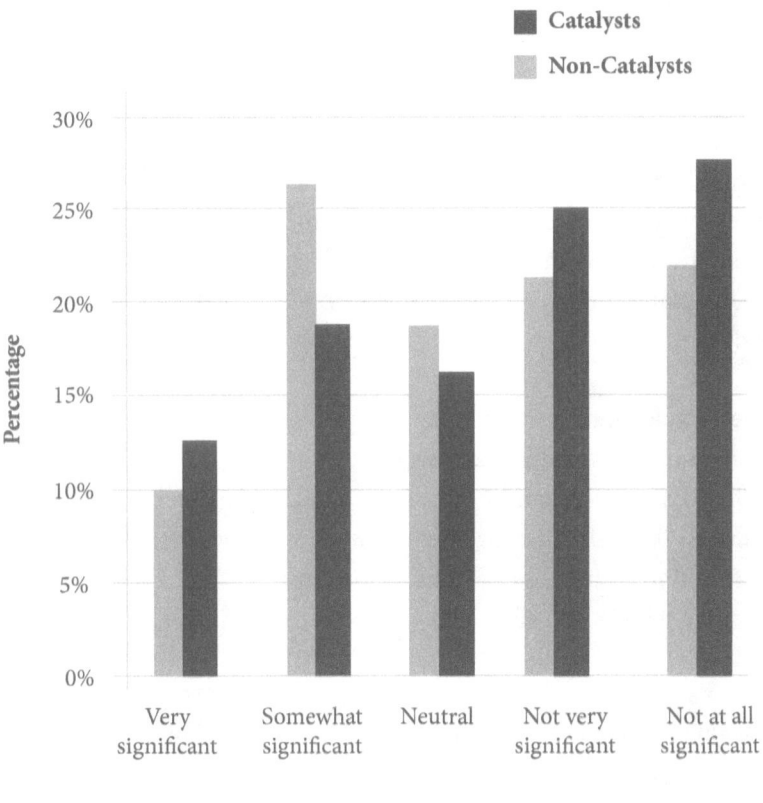

Figure 20.2: How Conversions without Human
Involvement Contribute to Movements

Figure 20.2 shows that "supernatural" conversions without human involvement are much less common than miracles in general. The results here are more similar between catalytic leaders and the control group. A pioneer in East Africa described the impact of dreams on his ministry:

Every time someone came to the church it was almost always because of having had a dream. For example, one man was a neighbor who had seen us meeting for three years. He had three dreams. In the first, he was climbing a coconut tree and fell off it. In the second dream, he was on his bed and his head was being cut off. Then, in the third dream, he saw a man in white—Jesus—who told him to come to him. Almost everyone in the church had had a significant dream.

In South Asia, a catalyst had been sharing the gospel with one family for some time and watched them "kind of inching toward faith." One of the sons, however, belonged to a radical fundamentalist Islamic movement and planned to kill the catalyst. He didn't follow through with his plan, and a year later, disillusioned with Islam, he saw Jesus in a dream:

> Jesus told him, "I have a gift for you and your family: People are going to explain it, and when they arrive, you must listen to them." The whole family ended up coming to faith because of that dream. They all came together: about eighteen or nineteen people, including some girls who had married in.... They just started telling people, and all we did was to keep studying Scripture with them.

Stories like this are very common: An individual has a dream, which ends up impacting his or her extended family and the wider community.

CATALYTIC LEADERS' PERSONAL EXPERIENCE WITH THE MIRACULOUS

The catalysts interviewed in one of my earlier studies, published in my book *Movement Catalysts*,[1] provided additional details about their personal experiences of the miraculous, which span a broad spectrum. Many said they have a miraculous gift and practice it frequently, while others reported that they don't have such a gift. Some even said that no miracles have happened at all in the entire catalyzing of their movement.

When miraculous experiences happen, they fall into four categories: prophetic words, supernatural revelations, miraculous answers to prayer, and dreams and visions. Catalytic leaders were asked to describe in what way their miraculous gifts had contributed to the catalyzing of their movement. Their answers can be summarized as follows:[2]

- Ministry strategy was revealed prophetically to the catalytic leader—especially how to pray and how to deal with ministry problems before they become obvious, so they can be addressed early and effectively.
- Miraculous answers to prayer in the name of Jesus provided evidence of the authority of the name of Jesus, demonstrating spiritual power in Jesus greater than that accessible to them, and making seekers want to join the movement.
- Miracles caused people to pray to God and even encouraged seekers to gather together to pray, which led to conversions and house churches being formed.
- Seeing prophecies fulfilled stimulated faith and boldness among believers.
- The catalytic leader's example (even if they only did a few miracles) led to local believers walking in miraculous gifting (often with more miracles).
- Dreams (for which the catalytic leader was praying) about the Bible or Jesus, or an instruction to meet an apostolic leader or local believer, led to seekers being convinced of the gospel.

The following example illustrates a number of these factors:

> The apostolic leader received a prophetic word from God to pray specifically for a miracle that would bring a particular family to faith in Jesus within twelve hours. The catalyst devoted himself to prophetic intercession. The next night someone in the family received a prophetic dream, which led the entire family to faith the next morning. In this family, a house church was started, and from this house church a movement began.

In some of the movements, miraculous gifts have played a very significant role, as shown by this example from Southeast Asia:

> In our network of now eleven movements, catalyzed by seven key nationals and myself ... the phenomenon of miracles widely

starts new clusters of groups. Last week at our quarterly retreat, we took a two-hour session to hear stories of miracles, and each of the ten people shared their stories, trying to limit themselves to two miracle stories each, but some slipped into telling three stories. Almost all the stories had the commonality that at least seven believer groups in three generations were spurred from one miracle.

The fact that a single miracle could lead to the establishment of seven new house churches, as a consistent pattern among ten different catalytic leaders, points to the significant role of this variable in the catalyzing of some movements.

The apostolic leaders who effectively catalyzed a movement, yet practiced miraculous gifts infrequently or not at all, gave the following rationales:[3]

- Although the apostolic leader did not practice a miraculous gift, local believers did. In contexts where the catalyst was an outsider, two reasons were given: (1) it promotes the health of the churches and demotes the outsider; (2) it demonstrates to local disciples that following Jesus is not only the religion of the outsider or foreigner.
- Catalytic leaders wanted the faith of believers to rest on Scripture, and wanted their focus to be on sin, repentance, and forgiveness, rather than on miracles.
- Miraculous gifts were not a significant part of the apostolic leader's personal tradition and theology.
- Miracles were necessary for the initial breakthrough, but not in the later stages of the movement.

Also, in many of these cases, apostolic leaders other than the primary catalyst reported practicing a miraculous gift among the people group, which contributed to the movement.

From Experience: "Small" Miracles Contributing to Movement Breakthrough Indirectly

In our own movement ministry, we have always sought opportunities to pray for people, including for healings and other interventions that could hardly be denied as divine. We have experienced miracles but not many, and they did not directly lead to immediate breakthroughs. However, they have indirectly contributed to the movement. I believe the fact that we prayed publicly for the sick was significant in establishing our spiritual identity and authority. The following example of a healing illustrates this.

The tribal chief walked toward me with obvious determination, while an elderly man who was at least seventy years old tried to keep up with him. "Aman [my Arabic name], you need to pray for Hussein here; [4] he is unwell." The chief had previously watched me pray for others who were sick. Obviously, he had sufficient faith to drag his friend to me from his straw hut at the other end of the village. When I asked Hussein what he needed prayer for, he rolled up his *jellabiya* (cloak) and pointed to sore skin all over his legs, adding that he had leg and back pain all over, and generally felt very frail. I thought, *Oh my! Lord, am I supposed to have faith that a fountain of youth will turn this old man into a bundle of energy?* But I prayed anyway. One week later, Hussein almost leapt toward me, this time with the chief trying to keep up. "Look, Aman, I am doing better. The pain is gone, and look at my skin!" He rolled up his garment again, this time showing that all the sores had disappeared! Neither Hussein nor the chief committed their lives to Jesus in response to the very obvious miracle. However, the story spread, and the belief that praying in the name of Jesus held power became deeply ingrained within the village community. The chiefs and villagers began to address me as *mawlana*, an Arabic title for a spiritual guide. They perceived me as such not only because I shared from the Holy Books with them, but also because I prayed publicly for the sick. That likely contributed to the movement breaking through a few months after this healing.

THE CORRELATION OF MIRACLES WITH THE CATALYTIC LEADER'S FAITH AND PRAYER LIFE

One possible explanation for the occurrence of signs and wonders is a connection with the traits of the catalytic leader. This conjecture is based on the theological conviction that God often performs signs and wonders in response to faith and prayer. (See, for example, Mark 11:22–24; Acts 4:30–31.) Indeed, catalytic leaders consistently manifest the traits of expectant faith and deep prayer. And the data reflects an association between these catalyst traits and occurrence of miracles. Scripture supports this connection. The miracles occurring in movements can be explained at least in part by the faith and prayer of catalytic leaders.

A GROWTH PATH TO CULTIVATE FAITH AND PRAYER

To grow in faith and prayer, you can take some specific steps gleaned from the lives of catalytic leaders.

- Meditate regularly on the Gospels and Acts, a practice that many catalytic leaders report to have bolstered their expectant faith for miracles.
- "Carry the bag" of someone with significant faith for miracles. Watch and learn from them and allow your faith to be challenged and inspired.
- Take steps of faith and offer to pray for people who are outside the kingdom. Even if no miracles happen, you have lost nothing; and you have demonstrated to someone tangible love and your spiritual identity.
- Regularly share testimonies of any miracles (small or large) among your team and partners, to see where God is already working, and to bolster your faith.

Maximizing Your Chapter Takeaways

Recap

- Miracles contribute significantly to movements—very significantly for 54 percent of catalytic leaders.
- Miracles occur more frequently in the ministries of effective catalysts than in the ministries of non-catalysts.
- Catalytic leaders rank six factors (out of eleven) as more crucial than miracles for achieving movement breakthrough.
- Some movements have been catalyzed without any miracles occurring, or they played only a minor role.
- We do well to follow the example of catalytic leaders' expectant faith and deep prayer life and pray for miracles—with conviction that miracles can contribute to movement breakthrough.

Reconnect

Pause for a minute, connect again in your heart with the Father, and pray: *Father, please show me how you want me to live out what I've learned in this chapter, so I can align with your ways and partner with you more fully. Amen.*

Record

- The key insights God has given me in this chapter are:

Reflect More Deeply

Use the following self-coaching questions for prayerful personal or team reflection:

- What has been our experience with miracles? Do we have any testimonies of miracles, small or large, that we can share among our team and partners?
- How actively and expectantly have I prayed for and sought miracles?
- How deep is my prayer life and how expectant is my faith? What is one step I can take to deepen my prayer life? What is one step I can take to bolster my expectant faith?
- Where can I take a step of faith and offer to pray for people outside the kingdom?

Realize

- I sense God nudging me to implement these key insights through the following action steps:
    - Action Step 1

    - Action Step 2

    - Action Step 3

ACKNOWLEDGMENTS

Tim Freeman, former Bethany International EVP, and Dan Brokke, retired CEO of Bethany International: You believed in the study underlying this book when only a visionary eye was able to see what could come out of it.

Bolthouse Foundation and another foundation that prefers to remain anonymous: You invested in BRI before we delivered any results.

The Bethany Research Institute team: Although I have authored this book, the underlying research was carried out by the entire team of the Bethany Research Institute at the time—Dr. Andrew, Alison Goldhor, a scholar who prefers to remain anonymous, and myself. Dr. Gene Daniels joined us later and contributed to the writing of the first drafts of chapters ten, fourteen, and fifteen. Alison Goldhor contributed to the first drafts of chapters three and twenty. All of you are world-class. Only as a team with the unique strengths of each of us were we able to pull this off.

Dave Coles: Your editing makes all my writings so much better, including this book.

Anna Robinson: Your developmental editing has made this book much more accessible.

My fellow movement authors Bill Smith, David Garrison, Stan Parks, Corey Hartman, Gene Daniels, Warrick Farah, Tim Martin, and Dave H.: You gave your valuable time and helpful input to the manuscript.

I feel deep, deep gratitude for each one of you! Without your contributions, this book wouldn't have come to be.

DEFINITIONS OF KEY TERMS

Movement: Following the standard definition of David Garrison, who defines a church-planting movement as "a rapid multiplication of indigenous churches planting churches that sweeps through a people group or population segment,"[1] a movement is defined in this study as "a rapid indigenous multiplication of disciples making disciples and churches planting churches in multiple streams within a people group to the fourth generation and beyond."

People Group: A people group is defined here as "the largest group within which the Gospel can spread as a church planting movement without encountering barriers of understanding or acceptance."[2] This is a missiological definition, on the basis of a biblical theology of "peoples."[3]

Pioneer: A pioneer is defined as someone who takes the good news to a previously unreached people group. It is the modern equivalent of the biblical term "apostle" (ἀπόστολος),[4] someone who is sent by the church cross-culturally to take the good news where it is not yet.[5] In recent years frontier missiologists have returned to the biblical term "apostle' or "apostolic leader."[6] These are equivalent to what is described here as a pioneer leader, a term chosen in order to communicate to a wider audience.

Catalyst: Missiologists commonly use the term "catalyze" to describe the way that the life and ministry of a pioneer can lead to a movement (as defined above).[7] A catalyst therefore is a pioneer who has played a role in initiating or growing a movement.

Effective Catalyst: A pioneer who has contributed significantly to starting a movement. In our study we defined effective catalysts based on two criteria: They (1) have catalyzed a movement with churches that have multiplied to the fourth generation, and (2) were the first to engage this people group with the gospel which led to the movement. He or she may not necessarily have been the first to ever share the gospel among the group but proved to be the most influential pioneer, even though others may have made significant contributions to launching the movement.

To describe a catalyst as "effective" therefore means that the pioneers themselves have an instrumental effect in initiating a movement. It does not mean that they are the only independent variable; therefore, rival explanations have been examined in the study.

Catalytic Leader: This term is used interchangeably with "effective catalyst."

Competency: McLagan defines a competency as "an area of knowledge or skill that is critical for producing the outputs."[8] In the context of this study, a competency is an area of knowledge or skill that is critical for the catalyzing of a movement. Within this definition, a competency is always set in relation to an activity or outcome, whereas a trait (definition below) is viewed by itself.

Trait: A trait is understood as a personal characteristic that contributes to consistent leadership effectiveness. Professor of psychology Stephen J. Zaccaro offers a helpful definition: "qualities that differentiate leaders from non-leaders" and include "motives, values, cognitive abilities, social and problem-solving skills, and expertise."[9] To clarify the relationship between traits and competencies, Robert Katz, an influential skills theorist, distinguishes the two: "Traits are who leaders *are*, competencies are what leaders can *accomplish*"[10] (both emphases his). Bernard Bass draws an insightful contrast in his definition of competency: "When traits are requirements for doing something, they are called 'competencies.'"[11] Within this definition, a trait is viewed by itself, whereas a competency may be that same trait set in relation to an activity.

APPENDIX I

Characteristics of Movements

David Garrison, "Universal Elements of CPM" (2004)[1]

- Extraordinary prayer

- Abundant evangelism

- Intentional planting of reproducing churches

- Authority of God's Word

- Local leadership

- Lay leadership

- House churches

- Churches planting churches

- Rapid reproduction

- Healthy churches

- High cost for following Christ

- Bold fearless faith

- Family-based conversion patterns

- Rapid incorporation of new believers

- Worship in the heart language

- Divine signs and wonders

- On-the-job leadership training

Alan Hirsch, "mDNA – missional DNA" (2006; 2016)[2]

- Lordship of Jesus

- Disciple-making

- Missional-incarnational impulse

- APEST culture

- Organic systems

- Liminality and communitas— outward-focused community

David Watson, "21 Critical Elements of DMM" (2008)[3]

- Passionate prayer and fasting

- Authority of Scripture

- Evangelize households/ families

- Empowering disciples

- Plan/be intentional

- Persons of peace

- Appropriate evangelism through discovery

- Groups

- Reaching out/mission

- Reproducing

- Inside leaders

- Authority and Holy Spirit

- Teaching obedience
- Training/mentoring/ equipping
- Compassion ministries

- Self-supporting
- Redeem local culture
- Communities of believers

- Persecution
- Spiritual warfare

Neil Cole, "Movement DNA (2010)[4]

- Decentralized empowerment
- Self-replicating units at every level
- Minimal organizational structure
- Independent of outside resources

- Driven by ordinary Christians
- Interdependent relationships
- Reproduction at every level
- Spiritual transformation of individuals

- Conversions of social networks
- Culture transformation

Steve Addison, "Characteristics of Movements" (2011; 2015)[5]

- Word
- Spirit
- Commitment to a cause (mission)

- White-hot faith
- Contagious relationships
- Adaptive methods

- Rapid mobilization
- Pioneering leadership

Robert Reach, "7 Root Principles of Church Planting Movements" (2016)[6]

- All Christians lead
- Immediate obedience
- Intentional reproduction

- Relational discipleship
- Passionate prayer
- Empowering through continual training

- Networking resulting in group conversions

24:14 Coalition, "Common CPM Outcomes" (2018)[7]

- Praying
- Scriptural
- Obeying
- Indigenous
- Holistic
- Rapidly reproducing

If we look for consensus, strictly speaking these seven leading descriptions only agree on a very few characteristics of movements. The characteristics with the most points of agreement are the Bible and its authority, reproduction, and prayer (if prayer is assumed in Addison's "white hot faith").

These authors would all agree on a few additional characteristics. Even if not highlighted in their published short lists of movement characteristics, they refer to them elsewhere in their writings. These characteristics include intentionality, disciple-making, obedience-orientation, church planting, and indigenous leadership. Although—with a lot of good will—a few more common characteristics might be identified, beyond these, the commonalities among authors remain relatively few.

This shows that movement researchers and thought leaders share a common, if somewhat limited, understanding of the characteristics of movements. Thanks to their work, we now understand what movements look like in their idealized form.

APPENDIX 2

Research Questions

The study sought to answer the following research questions:

- What are consistently stated traits and competencies of pioneers who were instrumental in catalyzing a movement?
- What are the traits and competencies that distinguish these effective movement catalysts from those who did not catalyze a movement?
- Which factors other than the pioneer's traits and competencies are consistently stated as contributing to or impeding the catalyzing of movements?
- What is the role of the pioneer's traits and competencies versus other factors (intervening variables) in the effective catalyzing of movements (or lack thereof)?

REPRESENTATIVE SAMPLE

The study sought to include participants representing the largest mega-cultures of the world, in terms of a combination of geography and religious affiliation, with a focus on the regions where most movements occur. The resulting sub-samples are as follows:

- Latin America
- Francophone Africa
- East Africa
- India
- Chinese Diaspora
- Indonesia

Surveys were translated into French, Hindi, Hindustani, Bahasa Indonesia, Swahili, and Spanish. In order to be able to run a range of statistical tests on the data set, our research team aimed at an absolute minimum of fifty respondents for effective catalysts, and a minimum range of 100–150 respondents for the control group of pioneers who did not catalyze a movement. In the end we were able to mobilize sample sizes of 147 for the effective catalysts and 160 for the control group, giving a total of 307 valid responses. We also conducted in-depth Zoom interviews with forty-five participants.

PARTICIPANT INCLUSION CRITERIA

All participants were pioneer leaders who had been engaged in church-planting ministry, with a vision to see self-multiplying churches planted.

Effective Catalysts: Pioneers qualified as eligible if they had catalyzed a movement, commonly defined as "a rapid indigenous multiplication of disciples making disciples and churches planting churches in multiple streams within a people group, to the fourth generation." Since more than one individual usually contributes to the catalyzing of a movement, a second set of inclusion criteria determined which pioneer qualified for the study. That person:

- had catalyzed a movement with fourth-generation churches; and
- was the first to engage the people group with the gospel which led to the catalyzing of the movement (not necessarily the first to ever share the gospel among them) and was the most influential catalyst (even though others may have made contributions to growing the movement).

For the control group, pioneers were selected if they:

- had been mainly doing church-planting ministry among the same people group for at least four full years; and
- had served in any of the six regions specified above.

RESEARCH DESIGN

Step 1: Construct Selection

Based on a review of the relevant literature on empirical leadership studies and apostolic and movement leaders, an initial list of thirty-three trait and competency constructs was reduced to twenty-four, grouped into three sections (Table A2.1)

Table A2.1: Trait and Competency Constructs, Grouped into
Three Sections or Domains

Section 1: Individual Traits and Competencies ("Big Five" Domain)	Section 2: Spiritual Traits and Competencies ("Spiritual" Domain)	Section 3: Social Influence Traits and Competencies ("Socio-Influential" Domain)
Radical Learning	Hunger for God	Extroversion
Innovation	Listening to God	Assertiveness
Drive to Achieve	Evangelistic Zeal	Inspiring Personality
Conscientiousness	Expectant Faith	Influencing Others' Beliefs
Personal Agency	Deep Prayer	Inspiring Shared Vision
Persistence	Tangible Love	Transformational Disciple-Making
Agreeableness	Confidence in Local Disciples	Empowering
Flexibility	Confidence in the Bible	
Emotional Stability		

We formulated five questions per item so that construct validity could be reliably measured.

Step 2: Cognitive Pre-Test

The clarity of the survey questions was assessed through cognitive pre-testing. The survey was initially administered to a group of nine, who were asked to provide feedback on question clarity, wording, etc. This resulted in multiple edits improving question clarity.

Step 3: Large Sample Pre-Test

Instrument validity and reliability were tested by means of a pilot survey completed by a total of 181 respondents. The pre-test comprised 120 questions (twenty-four trait and competency constructs with five questions each).

First, the research team tested the reliability of the survey instrument: the accuracy of measurements when these measurements are repeated. An instrument is reliable when all questions for a particular item fall within a close range.

Next, the team tested the survey instrument's validity: its ability to measure what it is supposed to measure (i.e., the right concept). This enabled us to identify survey questions that proved not to belong to the intended construct and should therefore be removed from the survey.

Based on the reliability analysis and the subsequent exploratory factor analysis, the final survey consisted of a total of forty-four questions related to twenty-four traits and competencies.

Step 4: Data Analysis of Online Survey Results

The online survey results were screened for validity. Responses were coded as relevant. The final data set contained 307 entries: 147 catalysts and 160 control group members.

ANALYSIS I: DESCRIPTIVE STATISTICS

After testing for reliability, we calculated several averages across sets of individual questions:

- Traits and competencies with more than one question were indexed by calculating the mean of all their questions. These are referred to as "trait and competency constructs."

- For the traits and competencies, the mean across all individual questions was calculated.
- An additional twenty-eight questions were designed to test for factors that were considered to have either boosted or blocked the successful catalyzing of a movement. In this case, the average was calculated of all boosting factors and of all blocking factors.

These boosting and blocking factors were also categorized as either internal or external factors. Internal factors were those under the direct or indirect influence of the pioneers and/or their team (for example, using the right ministry approach), while external factors were outside their control (for example, opposition from government or wider society). For this comparison, blocking factors were inverted so that all factors (blocking and boosting) point in the same direction and can be directly compared. Then averages were calculated for: a) all internal factors and b) all external factors.

The resulting descriptive statistical analysis featured average results for trait and competency constructs, both combined and separately, for catalysts and control group members. It also included cross-tabulations (pivot tables).

The descriptive analysis was complemented by inferential statistical tests to assess the representativeness of means differences. The Mann-Whitney U test is used to compare differences between two independent groups when the dependent variable is not normally distributed, in order to assess whether a means difference is statistically significant. The Kruskal-Wallis test assesses for significant differences on a continuous dependent variable by a categorical independent variable (with two or more groups). It is used for comparing two or more independent samples of equal or different sample sizes. For both tests, a test result (p value) of less than 0.05 indicates a statistically significant difference between at least one pair of results.

ANALYSIS 2: MULTIVARIATE ANALYSES

The research team conducted several regression analyses. A regression analysis measures the influence of a number of independent variables on an outcome variable, to see which of these factors influence the outcome in a significant way. In a normal regression, the influence of each factor on the outcome is measured separately. We ran logistic regressions in which the outcome variable is binary ("yes" or "no"). In our case, the binary outcome variable is that of effective catalysts who have catalyzed a movement, versus pioneers who have not done so and are therefore in the control group.

We only included those traits and competencies, boosting or blocking factors, and external or internal factors that had a statistically significant means difference between the catalysts and control group (measured through the Mann-Whitney U or Kruskal-Wallis tests).

Step 5: In-Depth Interviews

As with the search for survey participants, we sought to find interviewees representative of the largest mega-cultures of the world listed above. They were contacted through the research team's existing networks, which means that the sample is not necessarily representative, but it does provide a reasonable cross-section of people from different parts of the world. We were able to interview fifteen effective catalysts and thirty other pioneers for the control group.

The structured interviews consisted of fourteen open-ended questions, which allowed interviewees to share about their experiences while particularly focusing on the factors that had helped or hindered their fruitfulness. Interview variables that were quantitative or suited to quantitative analysis were coded.

Step 6: Synthesis of Findings

With 307 survey respondents and forty-five interviewees, we had a wealth of material to draw on for this study. The survey provided a broad range of information about each participant, and the interviews went into great depth, providing us with plenty of both quantitative and qualitative data.

Synthesizing the findings proved challenging because of differences between the two groups in terms of sampling, focus, and content. However, despite these challenges, useful comparisons can be made between data collected through the online survey and the interviews. While the statistics provide a broad framework for comparisons between catalysts and the control group, the interviews give glimpses into the realities of church planting and disciple-making in the participants' various contexts.

This systematic research design was carried out through academically rigorous analysis, prayerful individual reflection, and robust team discussion of the data. The data, findings, and conclusions form the foundation of this book. A complete description of the research methodology and a technical research report are available for download from www.catalyticleadership.info/resources.

NOTES

The Story Behind This Book

1. *Catalytic Leadership*; https://www.catalyticleadership.info/blog.
2. Ralph D. Winter says, "By the phrase 'all the nations,' Jesus was not referring at all to countries or nation-states. The wording he chose (the Greek word *ethne*) instead points to the ethnicities, the languages and the extended families which constitute the peoples of the earth." See "Unreached Peoples: Recent Developments in the Concept," *Mission Frontiers* 11 no 4 (1989): 18.
3. For example, Steve Addison's blog, *Movements*, https://www.movements.net.
4. Emanuel Prinz, "The Leadership Factor in Church Planting Movements: An Examination of the Leader Traits and Transformational Leadership Competencies of Pioneer Leaders Effective in Catalyzing a Church Planting Movement among a Muslim People Group" (doctoral dissertation, Columbia, SC: Columbia International University, 2016).
5. Emanuel Prinz, *Movement Catalysts: Profile of an Apostolic Leader* (Walsall, UK: Amazon, 2022).
6. Emanuel Prinz, *Exponential Disciple-Making and Church-Planting* (Bloomington, MS: Bethany International, 2019); available at https://www.catalyticleadership.info/training.
7. David Garrison, quoted in Prinz, *Movement Catalysts*, XIV.
8. If you are interested in more, you can find a technical research report on my website, https://www.catalyticleadership.info/resources.

Part One: Setting the Stage for Movements—Introduction

1. Emanuel Prinz, David Lewis, and Alison Goldhor, *Catalyst Competence Research: An Empirical Investigation into the Traits and Competencies of Effective Movement Catalysts and Other Factors Contributing to and Impeding Movements.* (Bloomington, MN: Bethany Research Institute, 2021, unpublished), 26.

1 Understanding the Movement Landscape

1. Prinz, Lewis, and Goldhor, *Catalyst Competence Research*, 26.
2. In social sciences, the term "tipping point" describes a critical moment when a small change triggers a big, and often irreversible shift in a system. Imagine a domino tipping over and causing an entire cascade of tiles to fall.
3. Justin Long, "How Long to Reach the Goal? Movement Engagements in every unreached people and place by 2025 (36 Months)," *Mission Frontiers* 45, no. 1 (2023): 34–37.

4. Justin Long, "How Long to Reach the Goal?" 35.

5. Gene Daniels, "How Exactly Do We Know What We Know About Kingdom Movements?" in Warrick Farah, ed., *Motus Dei: The Movement of God to Disciple the Nations* (Littleton, CO: William Carey Publishing, 2021), 58–67.

6. Warrick Farah, "Movements Today: A Primer from Multiple Perspectives" in Farah, ed., *Motus Dei*, 1–24.

7. For an excellent summary, see Warrick Farrah, "The Genesis and Evolution of Church-Planting Movements Missiology," *Missiology: An International Review* 50, no. 4 (2022): 349–361.

8. Jim Collins and Jerry Porras, *Built to Last: Successful Habits of Visionary Companies* (New York, New York: Harper Business, 1994).

9. Jim Collins, *Good to Great: Why Some Companies Make the Leap and Others Don't* (New York, New York: Harper Business, 2001).

10. David Garrison, *Church Planting Movements: How God Is Redeeming a Lost World* (Midlothian, CA: WIGTake Resources, 2004).

2 The Critical Role of the Catalytic Leader

1. Steve Smith, "A Profile of a Movement Catalyst," *Mission Frontiers* 36, no. 3 (2014): 38–41.

2. Steve Addison, *Pioneering Movements: Leadership that Multiplies Disciples and Churches* (Downers Grove, IL: IVP Books, 2015).

3. Trevor Larsen, *Focus on Fruit! Movement Case Studies and Fruitful Practices: Learn from Fruitful Practitioners*, A Toolkit for Movement Activists: Book 2 (n.p.: Focus on Fruit Team, 2016); Trevor Larsen, *Core Skills of Movement Leaders: Repeating Patterns from Generation to Generation*, A Toolkit for Movement Leaders: Book 7 (n.p.: Focus on Fruit Team, 2020).

4. Craig Ott and Gene Wilson, *Global Church Planting: Biblical Principles and Best Practices for Multiplication* (Ada, MI: Baker Academics, 2011); Gene Wilson, *Emerging Gospel Movements: The Role of Catalysts* (Eugene, OR: Wipf & Stock, 2021).

5. Prinz, *Movement Catalysts*; Prinz, et al., *Catalyst Competence Research*.

6. Wilson, *Emerging Gospel Movements*, 28.

7. David Greenlee, Sandra Menges, and Pradip Ayer, *A Selected Bibliography of Characteristics of Fruitful Church Planters and Movement Catalysts* (Operation Mobilization, 2023, unpublished), 6; David Greenlee, Sandra Menges, and Pradip Ayer, *Profiles of Vibrant Community Planters: What Can We Learn from Published Church Planter and Movement Catalyst Materials?* (Operation Mobilization, 2023, unpublished), 2.

8. Wikipedia, s.v., "Lone Ranger," https://en.wikipedia.org/wiki/Lone_Ranger.

9. Prinz, *Movement Catalysts*, 41–43.

10. John Maxwell, *The Power of Leadership* (Tulsa, OK: RiverOak Publishers, 2021), 37.

11. Alan Hirsch, *5Q: Reactivating the Original Intelligence and Capacity of the Body of Christ* (Atlanta, GA: 100Movements, 2017).

Part Three: Movement Boosters—Section Introduction

1. *Cambridge Dictionary*, s.v. "correlation," accessed January 14, 2025, https://dictionary.cambridge.org/dictionary/english/correlation.

2. My doctoral research; Prinz, *Movement Catalysts*, 103–104; New Generations, *Internal Qualitative Assessment (IQA) Code Book: Codes and Subcodes* (New Generations, unpublished, 2022).

5 Correlating Movement Booster #2—Leader Quality: Influencing Others' Beliefs

1. Bernard Bass and Ronald E. Riggio, *Transformational Leadership*, 2nd ed. (New York, NY and Hove, UK: Psychology Press, 2005).

2. Bass and Riggio, *Transformational Leadership*; Bernard M. Bass, "Two decades of research and development in transformational leadership," *European Journal of Work and Organizational Psychology* 8, no. 1 (1999): 9–32.

3. Phil Cooke, *One Big Thing: Discovering What You Were Born to Do* (Nashville, TN: Thomas Nelson, 2012).

4. Jim Wilder, *Renovated: God, Dallas Willard, and the Church that Transforms* (Colorado Springs, CO: NavPress, 2020).

6 Correlating Movement Booster #3—Leader Quality: Assertiveness

1. *Collins Dictionary*, s.v. "assertiveness," accessed February 11, 2025, https://www.collins-dictionary.com/us/dictionary/english/assertive.

2. Michael Sinclair, *A Vision of the Possible: Church Planting in Teams* (Pasadena, CA: Authentic Media, 2006), 6.

3. Prinz, "The Leadership Factor in Church Planting Movements," 155.

4. Robert J. House, Paul J. Hanges, Mansour Javidan, Peter W. Dorfman, and Vipin Gupta (eds.), *Culture, Leadership, and Organizations: The GLOBE Study of 62 Societies* (Thousand Oaks, CA: SAGE Publications, 2013).

5. Deanne N. den Hartog, "Assertiveness," in House, et al, *Culture, Leadership, and Organizations*, 427.

6. Ralph M. Stogdill, *Handbook of Leadership: A Survey of Theory and Research* (New York, NY: Free Press, 1974).

7. Stogdill, *Handbook of Leadership*, 81.

8. Robert J. House and Mary L. Baetz, "Leadership: Some Empirical Generalizations and New Research Directions," in Barry M. Staw (ed.), *Research in Organizational Behavior,* vol. 1 (Greenwich, CT: JAI Press, 1979), 399–401.

9. Robert Hogan, Gordon J. Curphy, and Joyce Hogan, "What we know about leadership. Effectiveness and personality," *American Psychologist* 49 (1994): 493–504.

10. Sinclair, *A Vision of the Possible*, 6.

11. Daniel R. Ames and Francis J. Flynn, "What Breaks a Leader: The Curvilinear Relation Between Assertiveness and Leadership," *Journal of Personality and Social Psychology* 92, no. 2 (2007): 307.

12. Ames and Flynn, "What Breaks a Leader," 318.

13. Copyright © 2007, American Psychological Association. Reproduced with permission. Ames, Daniel R., and Francis J. Flynn. "What Breaks a Leader: The Curvilinear Relation Between Assertiveness and Leadership." *Journal of Personality and Social Psychology*, vol. 92, No. 2 (2007).

14. Ames and Flynn, "What Breaks a Leader," 319.

15. Copyright © 2007, American Psychological Association. Reproduced with permission. Ames, Daniel R., and Francis J. Flynn. "What Breaks a Leader: The Curvilinear Relation Between Assertiveness and Leadership." *Journal of Personality and Social Psychology*, vol. 92, No. 2 (2007).

8 Correlating Movement Booster #5: Discovery-Group Approach

1. John Dewey conceptualized discovery learning as early as 1887 in *Psychology* (New York, NY: Harper, 1887); Jerome S. Bruner coined the term in "The Act of Discovery," *Harvard Educational Review* 31 (1961): 21–32.

2. Marvin B. Copenhaver, *Jesus is the Question: The 307 Questions Jesus Asked and the 3 He Answered* (Nashville, TN: Abingdon Press, 2014).

3. Philip W. Jackson, *Life in Classrooms* (New York, NY: Holt, Rinehart and Winston, 1968).

4. Robert W. Ferris, John R. Lillis, and Ralph E. Enlow, *Ministry Education that Transforms: Modeling and Teaching the Transformed Life* (Carlisle, CA: Langham Global Library, 2018).

5. Elliot W. Eisner, *The Educational Imagination: On the Design and Evaluation of School Programs,* 2nd ed. (New York, NY: Macmillan, 1985).

9 Correlating Movement Booster #6: Effectively Raising Up Leaders

1. Maxwell, *The Power of Leadership*, 31.

2. New Generations, *The Internal Qualitative Assessment (IQA) of New Generations* (unpublished report, 2021).

11 The Right Person With the Right Methods is What Starts a Movement

1. Garrison, *Church Planting Movements.*

2. Garrison, *Church Planting Movements*, 26.

3. David Watson and Paul Watson, *Contagious Disciple Making: Leading Others on a Journey of Discovery* (Nashville, TN: Thomas Nelson, 2014).

4. Watson and Watson, *Contagious Disciple Making*, 61.

5. David L. Watson, *Gemeindegründungsbewegungen: Eine Momentaufnahme*, 2nd ed. (Schwelm, Ger: Deutsche Inland-Mission, 2011), 114.

6. Watson and Watson, *Contagious Disciple Making*, 202.

7. Steve Smith and Ying Kai, *T4T: A Discipleship Re-Revolution* (Monument, CO: WIGTake Resources), 199.

8. Smith, "A Profile of a Movement Catalyst," 38–41.

9. Smith, "A Profile of a Movement Catalyst," 38.

10. David Watson and Paul Watson, *Contagious Disciple Making.*

11. Victor John with Dave Coles, *The Bhojpuri Breakthrough: A Movement that Keeps Multiplying* (Monument, CO: WIGTake Resources, 2019).

12. David Garrison, *Church Planting Movements.*

13. Steve Smith and Ying Kai, *T4T.*

14. George Patterson and Dick Scoggins, *Church Multiplication Guide Revised: The Miracle of Church Reproduction* (Pasadena, CA: William Carey Publishing, 2013).

15. Trevor Larsen, *Focus on Fruit! Movement Case Studies and Fruitful Practices: Learn from Fruitful Practitioners*, A Toolkit for Movement Activists: Book 2 (n.p.: Focus on Fruit Team, 2016); *Core Skills of Movement Leaders: Repeating Patterns from Generation to Generation*. A Toolkit for Movement Leaders: Book 7 (n.p.: Focus on Fruit Team, 2020).

16. Insider Ministry seeks to keep Jesus followers within their socio-religious communities. See Harley Talman and John Jay Travis (Eds.), *Understanding Insider Movements: Disciples of Jesus within Diverse Religious Communities* (Pasadena, CA: William Carey Library, 2006).

17. https://www.zume.training/about.

18. Nathan Shank and Kari Shank, Four Fields of Kingdom Growth: Church Formation Update (n.p.: NoPlaceLeft, 2015).

19. Neill Mims and Bill Smith, "Church Planting Movements: What Have We Learned?" *Mission Frontiers* 33 no. 2 (2011): 8.

20. Quoted in Addison, *Pioneering Movements*, 12.

21. Mims and Smith, "Church Planting Movements," 19.

12 Correlating Movement Blocker #1—Lack of Openness to the Gospel

[1] For more on the Dayton Scale, see Edward R. Dayton and David A. Fraser, *Planning Strategies for World Evangelization* (Eugene, OR: Wipf & Stock, 2003).

[2] Prinz, *Movement Catalysts*, 88–90.

[3] Leonard Marasculio and Ronald Serlin, quoted in Dwight McGuire, "2½ Percent: Church Planting Movement from the Periphery to the Center," *Evangelical Missions Quarterly* 46, no. 1 (2010): 24; Everett M. Rogers, *Diffusion of Innovations*, 5th ed. (New York, NY: Free Press, 2003).

[4] Frank Preston, "Media to Movements: A Disciple Making Movement Strategy," *Evangelical Missions Quarterly* 57, no. 2 (2021): 25.

[5] Smith and Kai, *T4T: A Discipleship Re-Revolution*, 83.

[6] Jerry Trousdale, *Miraculous Movements: How Hundreds of Thousands of Muslims are Falling in Love with Jesus* (Nashville, TN: Thomas Nelson, 2012), 155.

[7] Trousdale, *Miraculous Movements*, 161.

[8] Watson and Watson, *Contagious Disciple Making*.

[9] Rogers, *Diffusion of Innovations*, 17.

[10] McGuire, "2½ percent," 29.

[11] McGuire, "2½ percent," 29.

13 Correlating Movement Blocker #2—Busyness of Catalysts

[1] "Tentmaking" refers to the practice of supporting oneself financially through secular employment while also engaging in ministry activities. The term comes from the life of the apostle Paul, who was a tentmaker by trade and used his skills to support himself while he traveled and preached the gospel.

[2] Collins, *Good to Great*.

[3] This term was popularized by Charles E. Hummel in his book, *Tyranny of the Urgent* (Downers Grove, IL: IVPress, 1967; rev. ed. 1994).

[4] Stephen R. Covey, *The Seven Habits of Highly Effective People: Powerful Lessons in Personal Change* (New York, NY: Free Press, 1989).

15 The Personal Growth of Effective Catalysts

[1] Jay A. Conger, *Learning to Lead: The Art of Transforming Managers into Leaders* (San Francisco, CA: Jossey-Bass, 1992); Bernhard M. Bass and Ruth R. Bass, *The Bass Handbook of Leadership: Theory, Research, and Managerial Applications* (New York, NY: Free Press, 2008); Ellen Van Velsor, Cynthia D. McCauley, and Marian N. Ruderman, *The Center for Creative Leadership Handbook of Leadership Development*, 3rd ed. (San Francisco. CA: Jossey-Bass, 2010).

2. K. Anders Ericsson, Ralf T. Krampe, and Clemens Tesch-Roemer, "The Role of Deliberate Practice in the Acquisition of Expert Performance." *Psychological Review* 100, no. 3 (1993): 363–404.

16 A Journey Map for Growth

1. David Garrison, *A Wind in the House of Islam: How God is Drawing Muslims around the World to Faith in Jesus Christ* (Monument, CA: WIGTake Resources, 2014), 255.
2. Ericsson, et al., "The Role of Deliberate Practice".
3. See https://www.catalyticleadership.info/accelerator.
4. Gail Matthews, "The Impact of Commitment, Accountability, and Written Goals on Goal Achievement" (faculty presentation, Dominican University of California, no. 3, 2007), https://scholar.dominican.edu/cgi/viewcontent.cgi?article=1002&context=psych ology-faculty-conference-presentations.
5. Matthews, "The Impact of Commitment, Accountability, and Written Goals."
6. SMART is a mnemonic device coined by George Doran in "There's a S.M.A.R.T. Way to Write Management's Goals and Objectives," *Management Review*, Nov. 1981.

17 Assessing the Boosters and Blockers in Your Ministry

1. Garrison, *Church Planting Movements*, 171–198.

19 What's God's Job and What's Ours in Movements?

1. Gordon H. Clark, *Predestination* (Unicoi, TN: The Trinity Foundation, 2006); James I. Packer, *Evangelism and the Sovereignty of God* (Downers Grove, IL: InterVarsity Press, 2008); Jason W. Snyder, *Evangelism and the Sovereignty of God: How God's Irresistible Grace Compels Us to Share* (Dallas, TX: Dallas Theological Seminary, 2010).
2. Martin Luther, *Römerbriefvorlesung*, S. Borcherdt and Georg Merz (Eds.) (München, Ger: Chr. Kaiser Verlag, [1516] 1973); John Calvin, *Institutes of the Christian Religion*, trans. by Henry Beveridge (Grand Rapids, MI: Eerdmans, [1536] 1994); Wayne A. Grudem, *Systematic Theology: An Introduction to Biblical Doctrine* (Grand Rapids, MI: Zondervan, 1994).
3. Grudem, *Systematic Theology*, 315–337.
4. Jason Mandryk, *Operation World: The Definitive Prayer Guide to Every Nation*, 7th ed. (Colorado Springs, CO: Biblica Publishing, 2010), 95, 98; Jean L. Blanc, *Algérie, Tu es à Moi! Signé Dieu* (Thoune, Switz.: Editions Sénevé, 2006).
5. Mandryk, *Operation World*, 172, 557.
6. Grudem, *Systematic Theology*, 285, 286.
7. *Blue Letter Bible*, s.v. "ἀπόστολος," https://www.blueletterbible.org/lexicon/g652/kjv/tr/0-1/.

8. A number of commentators have interpreted "the day of the Lord" (referred to in the ESV as "the Day" in 1 Cor. 3:13) eschatologically as Jesus' second coming. Yet many other commentators see also a more temporal application of the testing and convincingly show that it refers to a day in time when what the minister has built is tested by trials [including Charles K. Barrett, *The First Epistle to the Corinthians* (Black's New Testament Commentary Series, London, Eng: A & C Black, 1968); F. F. Bruce, *The Epistle to the Corinthians* (Grand Rapids, MI: Eerdmans, 1986); Craig L. Blomberg, *1 Corinthians: A Commentary* (Nashville, TN: Broadman & Holman, 1994); and Gordon D. Fee, *The First Epistle to the Corinthians*, rev. ed. (Grand Rapids. MI: Eerdmans, 2014)].

9. Garrison, *Church Planting Movements*, 255.

10. Charles H. Spurgeon, "Sovereign Grace and Man's Responsibility," sermon delivered on August 1, 1858, at the Music Hall, Royal Surrey Gardens, London; quoted in his book *A Defence of Calvinism* (n.p.: CreateSpace Independent Publishing Platform, 2013).

11. Spurgeon, "Sovereign Grace and Man's Responsibility."

12. As a practical implication, practitioners may need to wipe the dust from their feet (see Luke 10:11), signifying in some culturally relevant form that the community's rejection of the gospel will have severe consequences for them. While still upholding that "the kingdom of God has come near to them/the community," the gospel messengers move on to reach a different, more receptive, population. The implication may be to keep evaluating, adjusting, and persisting among the overall non-receptive population and persist in identifying the 2.5 percent that are open. Such a decision, while informed by these biblical principles, can only be made in each and every individual situation by seeking God's guidance in prayer.

13. Greg Livingstone, *Planting Churches in Muslim Cities: A Team Approach* (Grand Rapids, MI: Baker Book House, 1993), 26.

20 What Role Do Miracles Play in Movement Breakthrough?

1. Prinz, "The Leadership Factor in Church Planting Movements" in *Movement Catalysts*.

2. Prinz, "The Leadership Factor in Church Planting Movements," 91–92.

3. Prinz, *Movement Catalysts*, 93.

4. Name changed.

Definitions of Key Terms

1. Garrison, *Church Planting Movements*, 21; Garrison, *A Wind in the House of Islam*, 39.

2. Joshua Project, "What Is a People Group?" quoted from the 1982 Lausanne Committee Chicago meeting, accessed July 12, 2021, https://www.joshuaproject.net/resources/articles/what_is_a_people_group.

3. John Piper, *Let the Nations Be Glad!: The Supremacy of God in Missions* (Grand Rapids,

MI: Baker Books, 1993); Richard Showalter, "All the Clans, all the Peoples," *International Journal of Frontier Missions* 13 (1996): 11–14.

4. Colin Brown, *The New International Dictionary of New Testament Theology,* vol. 1 (Exeter, UK: Paternoster Press, 1975).

5. Alan R. Johnson, *Apostolic Function in 21st Century Missions* (Pasadena, CA: William Carey Library, 2009).

6. Edward Murphy, "The Missionary Society as an Apostolic Team," *Missiology* 4 (1976): 103–118; Dan Greene, "Dusting off the Apostolic Function," *International Journal of Frontier Missions* 1 (1984): 15–21; Michael C. Griffiths, "Today's Missionary, Yesterday's Apostle," *Evangelical Missions Quarterly* 21 (1985): 164; David Fraser, "Frontier Missions: The Apostleship of the Abnormally Born," *International Journal of Frontier Missions* 3 (1987): 1–5; Larry W. Caldwell, *Sent Out!: Reclaiming the Spiritual Gift of Apostleship for Missionaries and Churches Today* (Pasadena, CA: William Carey Library, 1992); George Miley, *Loving the Church ... Blessing the Nations: Pursuing the Role of the Local Church in Global Mission* (Waynesboro, GA: Authentic Media, 2003); Michael Sinclair, *A Vision of the Possible: Pioneer Church Planting in Teams* (Pasadena, CA: Authentic Media, 2005); Johnson, *Apostolic Function in 21st Century Missions*; Don Dent, *The Ongoing Role of Apostles in Missions: The Forgotten Foundation* (Bloomington, IN: CrossBooks, 2011).

7. Alan Johnson, "Analyzing the Frontier Mission Movement and Unreached People Group Thinking. Part II: Major Concepts of the Frontier Mission Movement," *International Journal of Frontier Missions* 18 (2001): 89–97.

8. Patricia A. McLagan, "Models for HRD Practice," *Training and Development Journal* 43 (1989): 49–59.

9. Stephen J. Zaccaro, "Trait-based Perspectives of Leadership," *American Psychologist* 62 (2007): 6–16.

10. Robert Katz, "Skills of an Effective Administrator," *Harvard Business Review* 33 (1955): 40.

11. Bernard M. Bass with Ruth Bass, *The Bass Handbook of Leadership,* 103.

Appendix 1: Characteristics of Movements

1. Garrison, *Church Planting Movements.* Garrison also lists a few elements as occurring in most movements that I don't list in the table, as they are not characteristics of the movements, as such: a climate of uncertainty in society, insulation from outsiders, and suffering of missionaries.

2. Alan Hirsch, *The Forgotten Ways: Reactivating the Missional Church* (Grand Rapids, MI: BrazosPress, 2006); *The Forgotten Ways: Reactivating the Apostolic Movements* (Grand Rapids, MI: BrazosPress, 2016).

3. David Watson, *According to the Pattern: Church Planting Essentials - Critical Elements* (Unpublished, 2008).Watson also lists outside leaders and their function to model, assist,

watch, and leave; which I don't include in this in the table, as they are not characteristics of movements, as such.

4. Neil Cole, *Church 3.0: Upgrades for the Future of the Church* (San Francisco, CA: Jossey-Bass, 2010).

5. Steve Addison, *Movements that Change the World: Five Keys to Spreading the Gospel* (Downers Grove, IL: InterVarsity Press, 2011); *Pioneering Movements: Leadership that Multiplies Disciples and Churches* (Downers Grove, IL: InterVarsity Press, 2015).

6. Robert M. Reach, *Movements that Move: 7 Root Principles that Nurture Church Planting Movements* (St. Charles, IL: ChurchSmart Resources, 2016).

7. Stan Parks, Curtis Sergeant, and Steve Smith, "Movement Engagements in Every Unreached People and Place by 2025 (88 Months)." *Mission Frontiers* 40, no. 5 (2018): 38–40.

BIBLIOGRAPHY

Addison, Steve. *Pioneering Movements: Leadership that Multiplies Disciples and Churches*. Downers Grove, IL: IVP Books, 2015.

Ames, Daniel R., and Francis J. Flynn. "What Breaks a Leader: The Curvilinear Relation Between Assertiveness and Leadership." *Journal of Personality and Social Psychology*, vol. 92, No. 2 (2007): 307–324.

Barrett, Charles K. *The First Epistle to the Corinthians*. Black's New Testament Commentary Series. London, UK: A & C Black, 1968.

Bass, Bernard M. "Two decades of research and development in transformational leadership." *European Journal of Work and Organizational Psychology* 8, no. 1 (1999): 9–32.

Bass, Bernard M., and Ruth R. Bass. *The Bass Handbook of Leadership: Theory, Research, and Managerial Applications*. New York, NY: Free Press, 2008.

Bass, Bernard M., and Ronald E. Riggio. *Transformational Leadership*. 2nd ed. New York, NY, and Hove, UK: Psychology Press, 2005.

Blanc, Jean L. *Algérie, Tu es à Moi! Signé Dieu*. Thoune, Switz.: Editions Sénevé, 2006.

Blomberg, Craig L. *1 Corinthians: A Commentary*. Nashville, TN: Broadman & Holman, 1994.

Brown, Colin. *The New International Dictionary of New Testament Theology*, vol. 1. Exeter, UK: Paternoster Press, 1975.

Bruce, F. F. *The Epistle to the Corinthians*. Grand Rapids. MI: Eerdmans, 1986.

Bruner, Jerome S. "The Art of Discovery." *Harvard Educational Review* 31 (1961): 21–32.

Caldwell, Larry. *Sent Out!: Reclaiming the Spiritual Gift of Apostleship for Missionaries and Churches Today*. Pasadena, CA: Wiliam Carey Library, 1992.

Calvin, John. *Institutes of the Christian Religion* (trans. by Henry Beveridge). Grand Rapids, MI: Eerdmans, [1536] 1989.

Clark, Gordon H. *Predestination.* Unicoi, TN: The Trinity Foundation, 2006.

Cole, Neil. *Church 3.0: Upgrades for the Future of the Church.* San Francisco, CA: Jossey-Bass, 2010.

Collins, Jim. *Good to Great: Why Some Companies Make the Leap and Others Don't.* New York, NY: Harper Business, 2001.

Collins, Jim, and Jerry Porras. *Built to Last: Successful Habits of Visionary Companies.* New York, NY: Harper Business, 1994.

Comer, John M. *The Ruthless Elimination of Hurry.* Colorado Springs, CO: WaterBrook, 2019.

Conger, Jay A. *Learning to Lead: The Art of Transforming Managers into Leaders.* San Francisco, CA: Jossey-Bass, 1992.

Cooke, Phil. *One Big Thing: Discovering What You Were Born to Do.* Nashville, TN: Thomas Nelson, 2012.

Copenhaver, Marvin B. *Jesus is the Question: The 307 Questions Jesus Asked and the 3 He Answered.* Nashville, TN: Abingdon Press, 2014.

Covey, Stephen R. *The Seven Habits of Highly Effective People: Powerful Lessons in Personal Change.* New York, NY: Free Press, 1989.

Daniels, Gene. "How Exactly Do We Know What We Know About Kingdom Movements?" in Farah, W. ed. *Motus Dei: The Movement of God to Disciple the Nations.* Littleton, CO: William Carey Publishing, 2021.

Daniels, Gene, and Emanuel Prinz. "An Elusive Consensus: Traits and Competencies of Movement Catalysts." *Global Missiology* 20 (3) (2023): 33–45.

Daniels, Gene, and Emanuel Prinz. "Catalysts Are More Likely to Start a Movement the More They Grow." *Missiology: An International Review* 52 (2) (2024): 212–24.

Daniels, Gene, and Emanuel Prinz. "Movement Catalysts' Self-Awareness: A Factor in Fruitfulness." *Evangelical Missions Quarterly* 59 (4) (2023): 88–91. [https://missionexus.org/movement-catalysts-self-awareness-a-factor-in-fruitfulness/]

Dayton, Edward R., and David A. Fraser. *Planning Strategies for World Evangelization.* Eugene, OR: Wipf & Stock, 2003.

Den Hartog, Deanne N. "Assertiveness," in Robert J. House, Paul J. Hanges, Mansour Javidan, Peter W. Dorfman, and Vipin Gupta (eds.) *Culture, Leadership, and Organizations: The GLOBE Study of 62 Societies*. Thousand Oaks, CA: SAGE Publications (2013): 395–436.

Dent, Don. *The Ongoing Role of Apostles in Missions: The Forgotten Foundation*. Bloomington, IN: CrossBooks, 2011.

Dewey, John. *Psychology*. New York, NY: Harper, 1887.

Eisner, Elliot W. *The Educational Imagination: On the Design and Evaluation of School Programs*. 2nd ed. New York, NY: Macmillan, 1985.

Ericsson, K. Anders, Ralf T. Krampe, and Clemens Tesch-Roemer. "The Role of Deliberate Practice in the Acquisition of Expert Performance." *Psychological Review* 100 (3) (1993): 363–404.

Farah, Warrick. 2022. "The Genesis and Evolution of Church-Planting Movements Missiology." *Missiology: An International Review* 50, no. 4: 349–361.

Farah, Warrick. *Motus Dei: The Movement of God to Disciple the Nations*. Littleton, CO: William Carey Publishing, 2021.

Farah, Warrick. 2021. "Movements Today: A Primer from Multiple Perspectives" in Farah, W. ed. *Motus Dei: The Movement of God to Disciple the Nations*. Littleton, CO: William Carey Publishing, 2021.

Fee, Gordon D. *The First Epistle to the Corinthians*. Rev. ed. Grand Rapids, MI: Eerdmans, 2014.

Ferris, Robert W., John R. Lillis, and Ralph E. Enlow. *Ministry Education that Transforms: Modeling and Teaching the Transformed Life*. Carlisle, CA: Langham Global Library, 2018.

Fraser, David. "Frontier Missions: The Apostleship of the Abnormally Born." *International Journal of Frontier Missions* 3 (1987): 1–5.

Garrison, David. *Church Planting Movements: How God is Redeeming a Lost World*. Midlothian, CA: WIGTake Resources, 2004.

Garrison, David. *A Wind in the House of Islam: How God is Drawing Muslims Around the World to Faith in Jesus Christ*. Midlothian, CA: WIGTake Resource, 2014.

Greene, Dan. "Dusting off the Apostolic Function." *International Journal of Frontier Missions* 1 (1984): 15–21.

Greenlee, David, Sandra Menges, and Pradip Ayer. *Profiles of Vibrant Community Planters: What Can We Learn from Published Church Planter and Movement Catalyst Materials?* Operation Mobilization, 2023. (Unpublished.)

Greenlee David, Sandra Menges, and Pradip Ayer. *A Selected Bibliography of Characteristics of Fruitful Church Planters and Movement Catalysts.* Operation Mobilization, 2023. (Unpublished.)

Griffiths, Michael C. "Today's Missionary, Yesterday's Apostle." *Evangelical Missions Quarterly* 21 (1985):164.

Grudem, Wayne A. *Systematic Theology: An Introduction to Biblical Doctrine.* Grand Rapids, MI: Zondervan, 1994.

Hirsch, Alan. *5Q: Reactivating the Original Intelligence and Capacity of the Body of Christ.* Atlanta, GA: 100Movements, 2017.

Hirsch, Alan. *The Forgotten Ways: Reactivating the Missional Church.* Grand Rapids, MI: Brazos Press, 2006.

Hirsch, Alan. The Forgotten Ways: Reactivating Apostolic Movements. Grand Rapids, MI: Brazos Press, 2016.

Hogan, Robert, Gordon J. Curphy, and Joyce Hogan. "What We Know About Leadership: Effectiveness and Personality." *American Psychologist* 49 (1994): 493–504.

House, Robert J., and Mary L. Baetz. "Leadership: Some Empirical Generalizations and New Research Directions" in Barry M. Staw, ed. *Research in Organizational Behavior.* Greenwich, CT: JAI Press, 1979.

House, Robert J., Paul J. Hanges, Mansour Javidan, Peter W. Dorfman, and Vipin Gupta (eds.). *Culture, Leadership, and Organizations: The GLOBE Study of 62 Societies.* Thousand Oaks, CA: SAGE Publications, 2013.

Jackson, Philip W. *Life in Classrooms.* New York, NY: Holt, Rinehart and Winston, 1968.

John, Victor, with Dave Coles. *Bhojpuri Breakthrough: A Movement that Keeps Multiplying.* Monument, CA: WIGTake Resources, 2019.

Johnson, Alan. "Analyzing the Frontier Mission Movement and Unreached People Group Thinking; part II: Major Concepts of the Mission Movement." *International Journal of Frontier Missions* 18 (2001): 89–97.

Johnson, Alan R. *Apostolic Function in 21*st *Century Missions*. Pasadena, CA: William Carey Library, 2009.

Kai, Ying, and Grace Kai. *Training for Trainers: The Movement That Changed the World*. Monument, CA: WIGTake Resources, 2018.

Kasdorf, Hans. *Christian Conversion in Context*. Pawtucket, RI: Herald Press, 1980.

Katz, Robert. "Skills of an Effective Administrator." *Harvard Business Review* 33 (1955): 40.

Larsen, Trevor. *Focus on Fruit! Movement Case Studies and Fruitful Practices: Learn from Fruitful Practitioners. A Toolkit for Movement Activists: Book 2*. n.p.: Focus on Fruit Team, 2016.

Larsen, Trevor. *Core Skills of Movement Leaders: Repeating Patterns from Generation to Generation. A Toolkit for Movement Leaders: Book 7*. n.p.: Focus on Fruit Team, 2020.

Livingstone, Greg. *Planting Churches in Muslim Cities: A Team Approach*. Grand Rapids, MI: Baker Book House, 1993.

Long, Justin. "How Long to Reach the Goal? Movement engagements in every unreached people and place by 2025 (36 Months)." *Mission Frontiers* 45 (1) (2023): 34–37.

Luther, Martin. *Römerbriefvorlesung*. Edited by Borcherdt and Georg Merz. München, GER: Chr. Kaiser Verlag, [1516] 1973.

Mandryk, Jason. *Operation World: The Definitive Prayer Guide to Every Nation*. 7th ed. Colorado Springs, CO: Biblica Publishing, 2010.

Matthews, Gail. "The Impact of Commitment, Accountability, and Written Goals on Goal Achievement." *Psychology*. Dominican University of California Faculty Presentations (2007): 3. [https://scholar.dominican.edu/cgi/viewcontent.cgi?article=1002&context=psychology-faculty-conference-presentations]

Maxwell, John C. *The Power of Leadership*. Tulsa, OK: RiverOak Publishers, 2001.

McGavran, Donald A. *Understanding Church Growth*. Grand Rapids, MI: Eerdmans, 1970.

McGuire, Dwight. "2½ percent: Church Planting Movement from the Periphery to the Center." *Evangelical Missions Quarterly* 46 (1) (2010): 24–30.

McLagan, Patricia. "Models for HRD Practice." *Training and Development Journal* 43 (1989): 49–59.

Miley, George. *Loving the Church … Blessing the Nations: Pursuing the Role of the Local Church in Global Missions*. Waynesboro, GA: Authentic Media, 2003.

Mims, Neill, and Bill Smith. "Church Planting Movements: What Have We Learned?" *Mission Frontiers* 33 (2011): 8.

Murphy, Edward. "The Missionary Society as an Apostolic Team." *Missiology* 4 (1976): 103–118.

New Generations. *Internal Qualitative Assessment (IQA) Code Book: Codes and Subcodes*. New Generations, 2022. (Unpublished.)

Ott, Craig, and Gene Wilson. *Global Church Planting: Biblical Principles and Best Practices for Multiplication*. Ada, MI: Baker Academic, 2011.

Packer, James I. *Evangelism and the Sovereignty of God*. Downers Grove, IL: InterVarsity Press, 2008.

Parks, Stan, Curtis Sergeant, and Steve Smith. "Movement Engagements in Every Unreached People and Place by 2025 (88 Months)." *Mission Frontiers* 40, no. 5 (2018): 38–40.

Patterson, George, and Richard Scoggins. *Church Multiplication Guide: Helping Churches to Reproduce Locally and Abroad*. Pasadena, CA: William Carey Library, 1994.

Piper, John. *Let the Nations Be Glad!: The Supremacy of God in Missions*. Grand Rapids, MI: Baker Books, 1993.

Preston, Frank. "Media to Movements: A Disciple Making Movement Strategy." *Evangelical Missions Quarterly* 57 (2) (2021): 24–30.

Prinz, Emanuel. "DBS and Preaching: A Comparison of two Discipleship Tools." *Seedbed* 23 (1) (2022): 1–6.

Prinz, Emanuel. *Exponential Disciple-Making and Church-Planting*.

Bloomington, MS: Bethany International, 2019. (Available at https://www.catalyticleadership.info/training.)

Prinz, Emanuel. "The Leadership Factor in Church Planting Movements: An Examination of the Leader Traits and Transformational Leadership Competencies of Pioneer Leaders Effective in Catalyzing a Church Planting Movement among a Muslim People Group." Doctoral dissertation, Columbia, SC: Columbia International University, 2016.

Prinz, Emanuel. 2022. *Movement Catalysts: Profile of an Apostolic Leader*. Walsall, UK: Amazon.

Prinz, Emanuel, and Dave Coles. "The Person, Not The Method." *Mission Frontiers* 43 (4) (2021): 42–47.

Prinz, Emanuel, with David Coles. "Prerequisites for Movements? Questioning Two Widely-held Assumptions." *Global Missiology* 19 (1) (2022): 65–72.

Prinz, Emanuel, and Gene Daniels. "Charisma and Its Companions." *Christianity Today* 68 (4) (2024): 64–67.

Prinz, Emanuel, and Alison Goldhor. "Does the DMM Approach Lead to Movement Breakthrough?" *Global Missiology* 19 (1) (2022): 12–21.

Prinz, Emanuel, and Alison Goldhor. "The Effective Catalyst: An Analysis of the Traits and Competencies of Pioneers who have Catalyzed a Movement." *Global Missiology* 19 (1) (2022): 37–52.

Prinz, Emanuel, and Alison Goldhor. "The Kind of Person God Uses to Catalyze a Movement; Traits and Competencies of Effective Movement Catalysts." *Journal of the Evangelical Missiological Society* 3 (3) (2023): 60–73.

Prinz, Emanuel, and Alison Goldhor. "The Role of Signs and Wonders in Movement Breakthrough." *Global Missiology* 19 (3) (2022): 27–36.

Prinz, Emanuel, David Lewis, and Alison Goldhor. *Catalyst Competence Research: An Empirical Investigation into the Traits and Competencies of Effective Movement Catalysts and Other Factors Contributing to and Impeding Movements*. Bloomington, MS: Bethany Research Institute, 2021. (Unpublished).

Reach, Robert M. *Movements that Move: 7 Root Principles that Nurture Church Planting Movements*. St. Charles, IL: ChurchSmart Resources, 2016.

Rogers, Everett M. *Diffusion of Innovations*. 5th ed. New York, NY: Free Press, 2003.

Shank, Nathan, and Kari Shank. *Four Fields of Kingdom Growth: Church Formation Update*. n.p.: NoPlaceLeft, 2015.

Showalter, Richard. "All the Clans, all the Peoples." *International Journal of Frontier Missions* 13 (1996): 11–14.

Sinclair, Michael. *A Vision of the Possible: Church Planting in Teams*. Pasadena, CA: Authentic Media, 2006.

Smith, Steve. "A Profile of a Movement Catalyst." *Mission Frontiers* 36, no. 3 (2014): 38–41.

Smith, Steve, and Ying Kai. *T4T: A Discipleship Re-Revolution*. Monument, CA: WIGTake Resources, 2011.

Snyder, Jason W. *Evangelism and the Sovereignty of God: How God's Irresistible Grace Compels Us to Share*. Dallas, TX: Dallas Theological Seminary, 2010.

Spurgeon, Charles H. "Sovereign Grace and Man's Responsibility." Sermon quoted in Spurgeon's *A Defense of Calvinism*. n.p.: CreateSpace, [1858] 2013.

Staw, Barry M., ed. *Research in Organizational Behavior*, vol. 1. Greenwich, CT: JAI Press, 1979.

Stogdill, Ralph M. *Handbook of Leadership: A Survey of Theory and Research*. New York, NY: Free Press, 1974.

Talman, Harley, and John Jay Travis (Eds.). *Understanding Insider Movements: Disciples of Jesus within Diverse Religious Communities*. Pasadena, CA: William Carey Library, 2006).

Trousdale, Jerry. *Miraculous Movements: How Hundreds of Thousands of Muslims are Falling in Love with Jesus*. Nashville. TN: Thomas Nelson, 2012.

Van Velsor, Ellen, Cynthia D. McCauley, and Marian N. Ruderman. *The Center for Creative Leadership Handbook of Leadership Development*. 3rd ed. San Francisco, CA: Jossey-Bass, 2010.

Watson, David. *According to the Pattern: Church Planting Essentials—Critical Elements*. Unpublished, 2008.

Watson, David L. *Gemeindegründungsbewegungen: Eine Momentaufnahme*. 2nd ed. Schwelm, GER: Deutsche Inland-Mission e. V, 2011. (Only available in German.)

Watson, David, and Paul Watson. *Contagious Disciple Making: Leading Others on a Journey of Discovery*. Nashville, TN: Thomas Nelson, 2014.

Wilder, Jim. *Renovated: God, Dallas Willard, and the Church that Transforms*. Colorado Springs, CO: NavPress, 2020.

Wilson, Gene. *Emerging Gospel Movements: The Role of Catalysts*. Eugene, OR: Wipf & Stock, 2021.

Winter, Ralph D. "Unreached Peoples: Recent Developments in the Concept," *Mission Frontiers* 11 no 4 (1989): 18.

Zaccaro, Stephen J. "Trait-based Perspectives of Leadership." *American Psychologist* 62 (2007): 6–16.

ABOUT THE AUTHOR

DR. EMANUEL PRINZ has partnered with God to start a movement in North Africa and writes from personal experience. He has researched kingdom movements across the globe for fifteen years. Currently, he serves ministries worldwide as an expert movement consultant, coach, trainer, and researcher, facilitating their progression toward movements. Through his *Exponential Disciple-Making* and *MOVES Coaching* trainings, more than twelve thousand leaders in over fifty countries have been equipped.

Prinz has taught at Columbia International University, the European School for Culture and Theology, and Bethany Global University. He is the author of *Movement Catalysts* and numerous articles in journals such as *Missiology*, *Evangelical Missions Quarterly*, *Global Missiology*, *Journal of the Evangelical Missiological Society*, *Mission Frontiers*, as well as in *Christianity Today*. Above all, he seeks to live as the Father's beloved.

Prinz blogs at www.catalyticleadership.info.

PURSUING MOVEMENTS?

Benefit from the latest groundbreaking research.

Transform your ministry with actionable insights.

Subscribe today:

The Movement Catalysts Blog
www.catalyticleadership.info/blog

The Movement Catalysts Podcast
www.emanuelprinz.substack.com/subscribe

PURSUING MOVEMENTS?

Emanuel Prinz's mission is to boost ministries toward movements.

Services for Movement-Minded Ministries:

 Dynamic keynotes & transformational workshops for conferences & meetings

 Catalytic Leadership Accelerator – Online training cohorts for leadership teams

 MOVES™ – The Movement Coaching Training

 1-on-1 coaching for high-level organizational & movement leaders

Discover More: www.catalyticleadership.info

Apply Today: www.catalyticleadership.info/contact

EQUIPPING IN MOVEMENT MINISTRY

Multiplying Disciplers Training Platform
Online training for movement breakthrough

You are a movement practitioner? Need equipping that takes you to the next level in your movement pursuit? Our platform delivers just that. Short modules loaded with best practices – you select what you need, when you need it, from anywhere.

You are a leader? We offer to create tailor-made courses that meet your movement or organization's training needs. Let's talk!

Join our platform where movement practitioners get equipped, connect with others in an online community, sharpen and support each other, and have the option to share their own learnings and content.

Discover More: www.multiplying-disciplers.org

Register Your Interest: contact@multiplying-disciplers

What makes the Multiplying Disciplers platform unique?

- **Cutting-Edge**. Our content comes straight from the most thorough, in-depth research.
- **Proven Pathway**. We have equipped thousands of movement practitioners in these competencies.
- **Transformational**. We design all modules to transform thinking, spark passion, and reshape life and ministry practices.
- **Competence Building**. All modules contain actionable insights resulting in specific growth steps that build key competencies.
- **Top Quality.** Created by a world-class team of seasoned movement catalysts and leaders and educational experts.
- **Needs-Oriented**. You can select the modules you need, when you need them

BONUS MATERIALS
Exclusive Offers with Your Book Purchase!

SELF-ASSESSMENT VOUCHER

To **boost your personal growth** in becoming a catalytic leader, the **Catalyst Self-Assessment** will help you greatly. This tool affirms your areas of strength and highlights key areas for development. You will receive a personalized report with practical growth steps straight to your inbox.

We offer you a **$10 discount** on the Catalyst Self-Assessment.

Regular Price: $19   Your Price: Only $9

 Scan the QR Code and Enter BOOK25 to Claim Your Discount!

COACHING VOUCHER

Maximize the impact of the Catalyst Self-Assessment with a personal one-on-one coaching session. This energizing 45-minute coaching conversation will affirm your strengths, provide fresh clarity for your leadership journey, and help you identify the most valuable steps for growth.
Your coach is a seasoned and fruitful movement practitioner, trained and experienced in personal development coaching.

We offer you a **$40 discount** on a personal coaching session.

Regular Price: $100   Your Price: Only $60 This offer is valid until May 31, 2026

✉ **Email emanuel.prinz@gmx.net with the Discount Code BOOK25!**

ONLINE COURSE VOUCHER

We offer you a **$100 discount** on the course **What Actually Starts Movements: Factors that Boost and Block Movements and How to Leverage Them.**

Regular Price: $200   Your Price: Only $100

The course is part of the Ephesiology Master Classes – www.ephesiology.com/master-classes

We offer this voucher to give you the opportunity learn more about the factors that boost or block movements. The transformative insights can boost your movement toward movement.

Seize this opportunity to dive deep into the factors that make or break movements.

 **Scan the QR Code to Claim Your Discount!**